JOE CELKO'S SQL PROGRAMMING STYLE

JOE CELKO'S
SQL PROGRAMMING STYLE

Joe Celko

AMSTERDAM • BOSTON • HEIDELBERG • LONDON
NEW YORK • OXFORD • PARIS • SAN DIEGO
SAN FRANCISCO • SINGAPORE • SYDNEY • TOKYO
MORGAN KAUFMANN PUBLISHERS IS AN IMPRINT OF ELSEVIER

Publishing Director	Michael Forster
Publisher	Diane Cerra
Publishing Services Manager	Andre Cuello
Senior Production Editor	George Morrison
Editorial Assistant	Asma Stephan
Cover Design	Side by Side Studios
Cover Image	Side by Side Studios
Composition	Multiscience Press, Inc.
Copyeditor	Multiscience Press, Inc.
Proofreader	Multiscience Press, Inc.
Indexer	Multiscience Press, Inc.
Interior printer	The Maple-Vail Book Manufacturing Group
Cover printer	Phoenix Color Corp.

Morgan Kaufmann Publishers is an imprint of Elsevier.
500 Sansome Street, Suite 400, San Francisco, CA 94111

This book is printed on acid-free paper.

Library of Congress Cataloging-in-Publication Data

Application submitted.

ISBN: 0-12-088797-5

For information on all Morgan Kaufmann publications,
visit our Web site at www.mkp.com or www.books.elsevier.com

Printed in the United States of America
05 06 07 08 5 4 3 2 1

To Eve Astrid Andersson, Miss American π
And April Wilson, who rubs me the right way.

CONTENTS

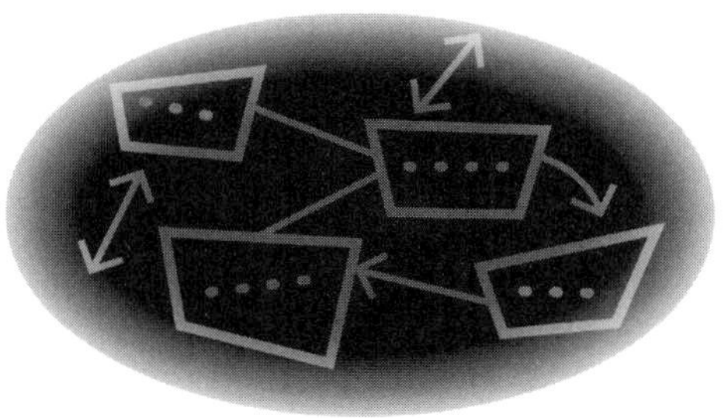

Introduction

I AM NOT trying to teach you to program in SQL in this book. You might want to read that again. If that is what you wanted, there are better books. This ought to be the second book you buy, not the first.

I assume that you already write SQL at some level and want to get better at it. If you want to learn SQL programming tricks, get a copy of my other book, *SQL for Smarties* (3rd edition, 2005). I am trying to teach the reader how to work in logical and declarative terms, instead of in a procedural or OO manner—"Query Eye for the Database Guy," if you will forgive a horrible contemporary pun.

Few, if any, SQL programmers came to SQL before learning and writing for years in a procedural or object-oriented language. They then got one particular SQL product and were told to learn it on their own or with a book that has a title like "SQL for Brain-Dead Morons," "Learn SQL in Ten Easy Lessons or Five Hard Ones," or worse.

This is absurd! It takes at least five years to learn to be a master carpenter or chef. Why would you believe people could become SQL gurus in a weekend? What they become is bad SQL programmers, who speak SQL in dialect from the local SQL product with a strong accent from their previous languages. You might want to read "Teach Yourself Programming in Ten Years" by Peter Norvig (www.norvig.com/21-days.html) or "No Silver Bullets" by Fred Brooks, *Computer*, 20(4):10-19, April 1987) to get a reality check.

The horrible part is that these people often don't know they are bad programmers. At one extreme, the entire shop where they work is just as bad, and they never see anything else. At the other extreme, if anyone tries to tell them about their problems, they become defensive or angry. If you look at postings on SQL newsgroups, many programmers just want to get a kludge for an immediate problem and not actually obtain a true long-term solution.

If these were woodworking newsgroups, their questions would be the equivalent of "What are the best kind of rocks to use to pound screws into fine furniture?" When someone tells them to use large chunks of granite, they are happy, but if you try to tell them about screwdrivers, they explode into a rage.

You might want to read an essay on this phenomenon: "Unskilled and Unaware of It: How Difficulties in Recognizing One's Own Incompetence Lead to Inflated Self-Assessments" by Justin Kruger and David Dunning (Department of Psychology, Cornell University, www.apa.org/journals/psp/psp7761121.html).

Or look at the actual and self-assessments of American high school students in mathematics and sciences that were part of the Bush administration's No Child Left Behind Act.

1.1 Purpose of the Book

So how did we old farts learn to be better programmers when dinosaurs walked the earth? One of the best helpers we had in the late 1970s when the structured programming revolution came along was a series of books entitled "[Pascal | FORTRAN | COBOL | BASIC] with Style: Programming Proverbs" by Henry Ledgard and some of his colleagues at MIT. The covers were done like a Victorian novel with angels, scrolls, and old-style typographical elements. And like a Victorian novel, the books were subtitled "Principles of Good Programming with Numerous Examples to Improve Programming Style and Proficiency." These books and others made a big difference for most of us because they taught us how to think like good programmers.

My goals in this book are to improve SQL programming style and proficiency. To be more exact:

1. *To help an individual programmer write Standard SQL without an accent or a dialect*. It is difficult to unlearn old habits but not impossible, and it is best to learn the right way from the start. Amateurs write code for themselves. A professional writes code

to be maintained and used by other people. My rule of thumb has been that you need to have a full year of SQL programming before you have your epiphany and suddenly see the world in three: valued logic, data models, and sets.

2. *To give an SQL shop a coding standard for internal use*. I have tried carefully to give a rationale for each of my rules, and I have given exceptions to those rules when I could think of them. You may disagree with some of my choices, but you will have to provide research and examples to defend your position. It is not good enough to simply declare: "Well, that's the way we wrote code in FooTran, so it must be the will of God!" as an argument.

   If you are the team leader, you now have a book (and author) that you can hold up and blame for anything that your people do not like. Even if I am later shown to be wrong about something, you will have been consistent. It is much easier to repair errors if they were made consistently.

3. *To give programmers the mental tools to approach a new problem with SQL as their tool*. I tell people it takes about a year to "get it" and drop your procedural programming habits.

1.2 Acknowledgments

Craig Mullins provided the structure of the chapter on VIEWs in an article in www.DBAzine.com. The formatting style is taken from a house style I have used in CMP magazines and other publications for more than a decade. Peter Gulutzan provided the data for the naming conventions in actual products from an article in www.DBAzine.com. The affix conventions in Chapter 1 are based on internal standards from Teradata Corporation. The scales and measurements and the encoding schemes material appeared in several of my old magazine columns in *DBMS* and *Database Programming & Design* before they were collected into a chapter in my book *Data & Database* (Morgan-Kaufmann Publishers). I have tried to give credit in the text, but so many people have participated in the newsgroups over the years that I know I am forgetting someone.

And, obviously, thanks to Henry Ledgard and his "Programming Proverbs" series for the inspiration.

I would also like to thank all of the newbie programmers who wrote bad code. It sounds a bit sarcastic, but it is not meant to be. Many of the

newbies are programmers who were thrown into a DBA or SQL programmer job by management without training or an experienced mentor. I do not want to blame the victims unless they are really not working on getting better. Your errors in syntax, semantics, and style showed me how you were thinking. Diagnosis is the first step to treatment.

1.3 Corrections, Comments, and Future Editions

Corrections and additions for future editions can be sent to Morgan-Kaufmann publishers directly or to me at my e-mail address, jcelko212@earthlink.net.

Names and Data Elements

This is the old joke:

"When I was a kid, we had three cats."

"What were their names?"

"Cat, cat, and cat."

"That sounds screwed up. How did you tell them apart?"

"Who cares? Cats don't come when you call them anyway!"

YOUR DATA WILL not come when it is called either if you do not give it a name that is always distinct and recognizable. This is an important part of any database project. Bad names for the data elements make the code difficult, or even impossible, to read.

I am not kidding about impossible to read. In the old days, software companies used to deliberately scramble source code names and remove formatting to hide the algorithm from the buyers. The tradition seems to linger on, even if not by intent. In August 2004, a SQL newsgroup had a posting in which all of the names were one letter and a long string of digits.

There are now ISO-11179 metadata standards that describe rules for naming data elements and for registering standards. Because they are an ISO standard, they are what you should be using in SQL as well as everywhere else.

That standard, a bit of typography, and some common sense will give you the rules you need to get started.

1.1 Names

In the early days, every programmer had his or her own personal naming conventions. Unfortunately, they were often highly creative. My favorite was a guy who picked a theme for his COBOL paragraph names: one program might use countries, another might use flowers, and so forth. This is obviously weird behavior even for a programmer, but many programmers had personal systems that made sense to themselves but not to other people.

For example, the first FORTRAN I used allowed only six-letter names, so I became adept at using and inventing six-letter names. Programmers who started with weakly typed or typeless languages like to use Hungarian notation (see Leszynski and Reddick). Old habits are hard to give up.

When software engineering became the norm, every shop developed its own naming conventions and enforced them with some kind of data dictionary. Perhaps the most widespread set of rules was MIL STD 8320.1, set up by the U.S. Department of Defense, but it never became popular outside of the federal government. This was a definite improvement over the prior nonsystem, but each shop varied quite a bit; some had formal rules for name construction, whereas others simply registered whatever the first name given to a data element was.

Today, we have ISO-11179 standards, which are becoming increasingly widespread, required for certain government work, and being put into data repository products. Tools and repositories of standardized encoding schemes are being built to this standard. Given this and XML as a standard exchange format, ISO-11179 will be the way that metadata is referenced in the future.

1.1.1 Watch the Length of Names

Rationale:

The SQL-92 standards have a maximum identifier length of 18 characters. This length came from the older COBOL standards. These days, SQL implementations allow longer names, but if you cannot say it in 18 characters, then you have a problem. Table 1.1 shows the maximum length for names of the most important SQL schema objects according to ISO and several popular SQL products.

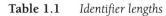

Table 1.1 *Identifier lengths*

	SQL-92	SQL-99	IBM	MS SQL	Oracle
Column	18	128	30	128	30
Constraint	18	128	18	128	30
Table	18	128	128	128	30

The numbers in the table are either bytes or characters. A maximum character length can be smaller than a maximum byte length if you use a multibyte character set.

Do not use super-long names. People have to read them, type them, and print them out. They also have to be able to understand those names when they look at the code, search for them in the data dictionary, and so forth. Finally, the names need to be shared in host programs that might not allow the same maximum length.

But do not go to the other extreme of highly condensed names that are impossible to read without weeks of study. The old Bachman design tool was used to build DB2 databases back when column length was limited to 18 bytes. Sometimes the tool would change the logical attribute name to a physical column name by removing all of the vowels. Craig Mullins referred to this as "Bachman having a vowel movement on my DDL." This is a bad approach to getting the name to fit within a smaller number of characters.

Exceptions:
These exceptions would be on a case-by-case basis and probably the result of legacy systems that had different naming restrictions.

1.1.2 Avoid All Special Characters in Names

Rationale:
Special characters in a name make it difficult or impossible to use the same name in the database and the host language programs or even to move a schema to another SQL product.

Table 1.2 shows the characters allowed in names by the standards and popular SQL products.

Generally, the first character of a name must be a letter, whereas subsequent characters may be letters, digits, or _ (underscore). Any database management system (DBMS) might also allow $, #, or @, but no DBMS allows all three, and in any case the special characters are not

Table 1.2 *Identifier character sets*

	Standard SQL	IBM	Oracle	Microsoft
First Character	Letter	Letter, $#@	Letter	Letter, #@
Later Characters	Letter, Digit, _	Letter, Digit, $#@_	Letter, Digit, $#_	Letter, Digit, #@_
Case Sensitive?	No	No	No	Optional
Term		Ordinary identifier	Nonquoted identifier	Regular identifier

usable everywhere (Microsoft attaches special meaning to names that begin with @ or # and Oracle discourages special characters in the names of certain objects).

But what is a letter? In the original SQL, all letters had to be uppercase Latin, so there were only 26 choices. Nowadays the repertoire is more extensive, but be wary of characters outside the Latin-1 character set for the following reasons:

1. *IBM cannot always recognize a letter*. It just accepts that any multibyte character except space is a letter and will not attempt to determine whether it's uppercase or lowercase.
2. *IBM and Oracle use the database's character set and so could have a migration problem with exotic letters*. Microsoft uses Unicode and so does not have this problem.

Intermediate SQL-92 does not allow an identifier to end in an underscore. It is also not a good idea to put multiple underscores together; modern printers make it difficult to count the number of underscores in a chain.

Exceptions:
None

1.1.3 Avoid Quoted Identifiers

Rationale:

This feature was added to SQL-92. Its main use has been to alias column names to make printouts look like reports. This kludge defeats the purpose of a tiered architecture. Instead, it destroys portability of the code and invites poorly constructed names. Table 1.3 shows the characteristics of delimited identifiers.

Table 1.3 *Quoted identifier character sets*

	Standard SQL	IBM	Microsoft	Oracle
Delimiters	""	""	"" or [ ]	""
First Character	Anything	Anything	Anything	Anything
Later Characters	Anything	Anything	Anything	Anything
Case Sensitive	Yes	Yes	Optional	Yes
Term	Delimited identifier	Delimited identifier	Delimited identifier	Quoted identifier

If you find the character-set restrictions of names onerous, you can avoid them by putting identifiers inside double quotes. The result is a delimited identifier (or quoted identifier in Oracle terminology). Delimited identifiers may start with, and contain, any character. It is a bit uncertain how one can include the double quote (") character. The standard way is to double it, as in "Empl""oyees" but that's not always documented.

Support for delimited names is nearly universal, with only two major exceptions: (1) IBM will not allow nonalphanumeric characters for labels and variable names inside stored procedures, and (2) Microsoft will not allow quoted identifiers if the QUOTED_IDENTIFIER switch is off. The reason for the first exception is, perhaps, that IBM converts SQL procedures into another computer language before compilation. Suppose you make a table with a delimited identifier, for example:

```
CREATE TABLE "t" ("column1" INTEGER NOT NULL);
```

Now try to get that table with a regular identifier, thus:

```
SELECT column1 FROM t;
```

Will this work? According to the SQL standard, it should not, but with Microsoft, it might. The reason is case sensitivity, which we discuss in section 1.1.4.

The quoted identifiers do not work well with hot languages, especially when they have spaces or special characters. For example, this is a valid insertion statement:

```
INSERT INTO Table ([field with space]) VALUES (value);
```

ADO generates the following code:

```
INSERT INTO Table (field with space) VALUES (value);
```

which is a syntax error.

Exceptions:
If you need to communicate a result to someone who cannot read or understand the properly constructed column names in Latin-1, then use quoted aliases to format the output. I have done this for Polish and Chinese speakers.

I also use quoted names inside documentation so that they will immediately read as the name of a schema object and not a regular word in the sentence.

The usual reason for this error is that the programmer confuses a data element name with a display header. In traditional procedural languages, the data file and the application are in the same tier; in SQL, the database is totally separate from the front end where the data is displayed.

1.1.4 Enforce Capitalization Rules to Avoid Case-Sensitivity Problems

Rationale:
Case-sensitivity rules vary from product to product.

Standard SQL, IBM, and Oracle will convert regular identifiers to uppercase but will not convert delimited identifiers to uppercase. For Microsoft, the case-sensitivity rule has nothing to do with whether the name is regular or delimited. Instead, identifiers depend on the default collation. If the default collation is case insensitive, then t equals T. If it's case sensitive, then t does not equal T.

To sum up, there are two case-sensitivity problems. The first is that the delimited identifier "t" and the regular identifier t differ if one follows the SQL standard. The second is that Microsoft does not follow the SQL standard. These problems make it difficult for one naming convention to fit everyone.

Exceptions:
I will give a simple set of rules based on principles of readability and typography, but there are other possible conventions:

1. Avoid delimited identifiers so you have no problems.
2. IBM uses only uppercase. Unfortunately, this is difficult to read and looks like you are still programming on a punchcard system.
3. Microsoft and Oracle use lowercase except where it would look odd. Unfortunately, the definition of looking odd is not at all precise. Sometimes reserved words are uppercased, sometimes lowercased, and so forth.

1.2 Follow the ISO-11179 Standards Naming Conventions

This is a fairly new ISO standard for metadata, and it is not well understood. Fortunately, the parts that a SQL programmer needs to know are pretty obvious and simple. The real problem is in the many ways that people violate them. A short summary of the NCITS L8 Metadata Standards Committee rules for data elements can be found at the following sites:

`http://pueblo.lbl.gov/~olken/X3L8/drafts/draft.docs.html`
`http://lists.oasis-open.org/archives/ubl-ndrsc/200111/msg00005.html`

Also the pdf file:
`www.oasis-open.org/committees/download.php/6233/c002349_ISO_IEC_11179`

and the draft:
`www.iso.org/iso/en/ittf/PubliclyAvailableStandards/c002349_ISO_IEC_11179-1_1999(E).zip`

The ISO-11179 standard is broken down into six sections:

```
11179-1: Framework for the Specification and Standardization of
Data Elements Definitions
11179-2: Classification for Data Elements
11179-3: Basic Attributes of Data Elements
11179-4: Rules and Guidelines for the Formulation of Data
11179-5: Naming and Identification Principles for Data
11179-6: Registration of Data Elements
```

1.2.1 ISO-11179 for SQL

Rationale:

Although the formal standards are good, they are very general. It is handy to have a set of rules aimed at the SQL developer in his or her own language. Some of the interpretations given here are the consensus of experts, as taken from newsgroups and private e-mails.

Taking the rules from Section ISO-11179-4, a scalar data element should do the following:

1. Be unique (within any data dictionary in which it appears).
2. Be stated in the singular.
3. State what the concept is, not only what it is not.
4. Be stated as a descriptive phrase or sentence(s).
5. Contain only commonly understood abbreviations.
6. Be expressed without embedding definitions of other data elements or underlying concepts.
7. Tables, sets, and other collections shall be named with a collective, class, or plural name.
8. Procedures shall have a verb in their name.
9. A copy (alias) of a table shall include the base table name as well as the role it is playing at that time.

This formalism is nice in theory, but names are subject to constraints imposed by software limitations in the real world, such as maximum name length and character sets. Another problem is that one data element may have many names depending on the context in which it is used. It might be called something in a report and something else in an electronic data interchange (EDI) file, and it might be different from the name in the database. But you want to avoid using multiple names in the same database, and you should be able to detect them with metadata tools. Furthermore, you want to avoid using multiple names in different databases in the same enterprise. Unfortunately, this is much more difficult to detect without very good data dictionary tools. The data dictionary should include the external names and their context.

Exceptions:
The curse of legacy databases, legacy file systems, and other traditions can make this very difficult. If there is a common, well-understood name for a data element, then you can use this name instead of a constructed name. For example, "us_postal_code" is formally correct, but "zip_code" is well understood, and you can argue for simply "zip" or "zip4" as a name because it is a familiar term.

1.2.2 Levels of Abstraction

Name development begins at the conceptual level. An object class represents an idea, abstraction, or thing in the real world, such as tree or country. A property is something that describes all objects in the class, such as height or identifier. This lets us form terms such as "tree height" or "country identifier" from the combination of the class and the property.

The level in the process is the logical level. A complete logical data element must include a form of representation for the values in its data value domain (the set of possible valid values of a data element). The representation term describes the data element's representation class. The representation class is equivalent to the class word of the prime/class naming convention with which many data administrators are familiar. This gets us to "tree height measure," "country identifier name," and "country identifier code" as possible data elements.

There is a subtle difference between "identifier name" and "identifier code," and it might be so subtle that we do not want to model it, but we would need a rule to drop the property term in this case. The property would still exist as part of the inheritance structure of the data element, but it would not be part of the data element name.

Some logical data elements can be considered generic elements if they are well defined and are shared across organizations. Country names and country codes are well defined in the ISO 3166 standard, "Codes for the Representation of Names of Countries," and you might simply reference this document.

Note that this is the highest level at which true data elements, by the definition of ISO-11179, appear: They have an object class, a property, and a representation.

The next is the application level. This is usually done with a quantifier that applies to the particular application. The quantifier will either subset the data value domain or add more restrictions to the definition so that we work with only those values needed in the application.

For example, assume that we are using ISO-3166 country codes, but we are only interested in Europe. This would be a simple subset of the standard, but it will change slowly over time. However, the subset of countries with more than 20 centimeters of rain this year will vary greatly in a matter of weeks.

Changes in the name to reflect this fact will be accomplished by addition of qualifier terms to the logical name. For example, if a view were to list all of the countries with which a certain organization had trading agreements, the query data element might be called "trading_partner_country_name" to show its role in the context of the VIEW or query that limits it. The data value domain would consist of a subset of countries listed in ISO-3166.

The physical name is the lowest level. These are the names that actually appear in the database table column headers, file descriptions, EDI transaction file layouts, and so forth. They may be abbreviations or use a limited character set because of software restrictions. However, they might also add information about their origin or format.

In a registry, each of the data element names and name components will always be paired with its context so that we know the source or usage of the name or name component. The goal is to be able to trace each data element from its source to wherever it is used, regardless of the name under which it appears.

1.2.3 Avoid Descriptive Prefixes

Rationale:

Another silly convention among newbies is to use prefixes that describe something about the appearance of the data element in the current table. In the old days, when we worked with sequential file systems, the physical location of the file was very important.

The "tbl-" prefix is particularly silly. Before you counter that this prefix answers the question of what something is, remember that SQL has only one data structure. What else could it be? Do you put "n-" in front of every noun you write? Do you think this would make English easier to read? It is like infants announcing that everything is "thingie!" as they grab them.

> "*To be something is to be something in particular; to be nothing in particular or anything in general is to be nothing.*" —Aristotle

The next worst affix is the <table name>. Why does a data element become something totally different from table to table? For example, "orders_upc" and "inventory_upc" are both UPC codes no matter where they appear, but by giving them two names, you are saying that they are totally, logically different things in your data model.

A total nightmare is the combination of "id" in a base table (vague name) with a reference in a second table using the base table name as a prefix in the foreign key or non-foreign-key references. The queries fill up with code like "Orders.ID = OrderID," which quickly becomes a game of looking for the period and trying to figure out what a thousand different "ID" columns mean in the data dictionary.

Affixes like "vw" for views tell you how the virtual table is implemented in the schema, but this has nothing to do with the data model. If I later decide to replace the view with a base table, do I change the name? The bad news is that a table often already exists with the same root name, which makes for more confusion.

Equally silly and dangerous are column names that are prefixed with the data type. This is how it is physically represented and not what it means in the data model. The data dictionary will be trashed, because you have no idea if there are "intorder_nbr," "strorder_nbr," and perhaps even "forder_nbr," all trying to be the simple "order_nbr" at the same time. The user can also look at the data declaration language (DDL) and see the data type, defaults, and constraints if he or she does not remember them.

The final affix problem is telling us that something is the primary key with a "PK_" or a foreign key with an "FK_" affix. That is how it is used in that particular table; it is not a part of its fundamental nature. The user can also look at the DDL and see the words "PRIMARY KEY" or "FOREIGN KEY.. REFERENCES.." in the column declarations.

The strangest version of this is a rule on a Web site for a company that specializes in Oracle programming. It advocated "<table name>_CK_<column name>" for CHECK() constraints. This not only gives you no help in determining the errors that caused the violation, but it also limits you to one and only one constraint per column per table, and it leaves you to ask about constraints that use two or more columns.

The same rules and warnings about affixes apply to all schema objects. You will see "usp_" for user-defined stored procedures, "trig_" for triggers, and so forth. In MS SQL Server, this is a serious problem, because the prefix "sp_" is used for system procedures and has special meaning in the architecture.

If the schema object does something (triggers, procedures), then use a <verb><object> format for the name; the subject of the sentence is understood to be the procedure. We will go into more details on this topic in Chapter 8.

Exceptions:

You can find other opinions at:

`http://www.craigsmullins.com/dbt_0999.htm`

There was also a series of articles at:

`http://www.sqlservercentral.com/columnists/sjones/codingstandardspart2formatting.asp`

`http://www.sqlservercentral.com/columnists/sjones/codingstandardspart1formatting.asp`

1.2.4 Develop Standardized Postfixes

This list of postfixes is built on Teradata's internal standards and common usage. The Teradata standards are given in the Appendix.

"_id" = identifier. It is unique in the schema and refers to one entity anywhere it appears in the schema. Never use "<table name>_id"; that is a name based on location and tells you this is probably not a real key at all. Just plain "id" is too vague to be useful to anyone and will screw up your data dictionary when you have to find a zillion of them, all different, but with the same data element name and perhaps the same oversized data type.

"_date" or "dt" = date, temporal dimension. It is the date of something—employment, birth, termination, and so forth; there is no such column name as just a date by itself.

"_nbr" or "num" = tag number. This is a string of digits that names something. Do not use "_no" because it looks like the Boolean yes/no value. I prefer "nbr" to "num" because it is used as a common abbreviation in several European languages.

"_name" or "nm" = alphabetic name. This explains itself. It is also called a nominal scale.

"_code" or "_cd" = a code is a standard maintained by a trusted source, usually outside of the enterprise. For example, the ZIP code is maintained by the U.S. Postal Service. A code is well understood in its context, so you might not have to translate it for humans.

"_size" = an industry standard or company scale for a commodity, such as clothing, shoes, envelopes, or machine screws. There is usually a prototype that defines the sizes kept with a trusted source.

"_tot" = a sum, an aggregated dimension that is logically different from its parts.

"_seq" = sequence, ordinal numbering. This is not the same thing as a tag number, because it cannot have gaps.

"_tally" = a count of values. Also called an absolute scale.

"_cat" = category, an encoding that has an external source that has distinct groups of entities. There should be strong, formal criteria for establishing the category. The classification of Kingdom in Biology is an example.

"_class" = an internal encoding that does not have an external source that reflects a subclassification of the entity. There should be strong formal criteria for the classification. The classification of plants in Biology is an example.

"_type" = an encoding that has a common meaning both internally and externally. Types are usually less formal than a class and might overlap. For example, a driver's license might be typed for motorcycles, automobiles, taxis, trucks, and so forth.

The differences among type, class, and category are an increasing strength of the algorithm for assigning the type, class, or category. A category is distinct; you will not often have to guess if something is animal, vegetable, or mineral to put it in one of those categories.

A class is a set of things that have some commonality; you have rules for classifying an animal as a mammal or a reptile. You may have some cases for which it is more difficult to apply the rules, such as the platypus, an egg-laying mammal that lives in Australia, but the exceptions tend to become their own classification—monotremes in this example.

A type is the weakest of the three, and it might call for a judgment. For example, in some states a three-wheeled motorcycle is licensed as a

motorcycle, but in other states, it is licensed as an automobile, and in some states, it is licensed as an automobile only if it has a reverse gear.

The three terms are often mixed in actual usage. Stick with the industry standard, even if it violates the aforementioned definitions.

> "_status" = an internal encoding that reflects a state of being, which can be the result of many factors. For example, "credit_status" might be computed from several sources.
>
> "_addr" or "_loc" = an address or location for an entity. There can be a subtle difference between an address and a location.
>
> "_img" = an image data type, such as .jpg, .gif, and so forth.

Then an application might have some special situations with units of measurement that need to be shown on an attribute or dimension. And *always* check to see if there is an ISO standard for a data element.

1.2.5 Table and View Names Should Be Industry Standards, Collective, Class, or Plural Nouns

Rationale:

Industry standards should always be used. People in that industry will understand the name, and the definition will be maintained by the organization that sets those standards.

For example, the North American Industry Classification System (NAICS) has replaced the old Standard Industrial Classification (SIC) system in the United States. This new code was developed jointly by the United States, Canada, and Mexico to provide new comparability in statistics about business activity across North America. The names "NAICS" and "naics_code" are clear to people who do business statistics, even though they look weird to the rest of us.

If an industry standard is not right for your situation, then try to base your names on that standard. For example, if I am dealing only with automobiles made in Mexico, I could have a table named "VIN_Mexico" to show the restriction. Moving down the priority list, if I cannot find an industry standard, I would look for a collective or class name. I would never use a singular name.

Collective or class table names are better than singular names because a table is a set and not a scalar value. If I say "Employee," the mental picture is of Dilbert standing by himself—one generic employee. If I say "Employees," the mental picture is of the crew from Dilbert—a collection of separate employees. If I say "Personnel," the mental picture is suddenly more abstract—a class without particular faces on it.

It is legal in SQL to give a table and a column the same name, but it is a really bad idea. First of all, the column's name would be in violation of the rules we just discussed because it would lack a qualifier, but it would also mean that either the table name is not a set or the column name is not a scalar.

Exceptions:
Use a singular name if the table actually has one and only one row in it. The one example I can think of is a table for constants that looks like this:

```
CREATE TABLE Constant
(lock CHAR(1) DEFAULT 'X' NOT NULL PRIMARY KEY
      CHECK (lock = 'X'),
 pi  REAL DEFAULT 3.141592653 NOT NULL,
 e REAL DEFAULT 2.718281828 NOT NULL,
 phi REAL DEFAULT 1.618033988 NOT NULL,
 ..);

INSERT INTO Constants DEFAULT VALUES;
```

The insertion creates one row, so the table ought to have a singular name. The "lock" column assures you that there is always only one row. Another version of this is to create a VIEW that cannot be changed using SQL-99 syntax.

```
CREATE VIEW Constant (pi, e, phi, ..)
AS VALUES (3.141592653, 2.718281828, 1.618033988, ..);
```

The advantage is that this view cannot be changed; the disadvantage is that this view cannot be changed.

1.2.6 Correlation Names Follow the Same Rules as Other Names . . . Almost

Rationale:
Correlation names are names. They should be derived from the base table or view name, the column name, or from the expression that

creates them. The nice part is that the readers have the context in front of them, so you can often use a more abbreviated name.

A correlation name is more often called an *alias*, but I will be formal. In SQL-92, they can have an optional AS operator, and it should be used to make it clear that something is being given a new name.

This explicitly means that you do not use an alphabetical sequence unrelated to the base table name. This horrible practice is all too common and makes maintaining the code much more difficult. Consider looking at several statements where the table "Personnel" is aliased as "A" in one, "D" in another, and "Q" in a third because of its position in a FROM clause.

Column correlation names for a computed data element should name the computed data element in the same way that you would name a declared column. That is, try to find a common term for the computation. For example, "salary + COALESCE(commission, 0.00)) AS total_pay" makes sense to the reader.

A simple table or view correlation name should have a short, simple name derived from the base table name or descriptive of the role that copy of the table is playing in the statement (e.g., "SELECT .. FROM Personnel AS Management, Personnel AS Workers" as the two uses of the table in the query).

Now to explain the "almost" part of this section's title. In the case of multiple correlation names on the same table, you may find it handy to postfix abbreviated names with a number (e.g., "SELECT .. FROM Personnel AS P1, Personnel AS P2"). The digit is to tell the reader how many correlation names are used in the statement for that table.

In effect, these are "correlation pronouns"—a shorthand that makes sense in a local context. They are used for the same reason as pronouns in a natural language: to make the statement shorter and easier to read.

A table expression alias should have a short, simple name derived from the logical meaning of the table expression.

```
SELECT  ..
  FROM (Personnel AS P1
        INNER JOIN
        SoftballTeams AS S1
        ON P1.ssn = S1.ssn) AS CompanyTeam (..)
        ..
 WHERE ..;
```

Although not required, the correlation name on a table expression can be followed by a list of new column names in parentheses. If this list is missing, the correlation name inherits the names from the base tables or views in the table expression. In the case of a simple table correlation name, such a list would probably be redundant because we usually want to use the original column names.

In the case of a table expression correlation name, such a list would probably be a good idea to avoid ambiguous column names. It also forces the programmer to trim the expression of extraneous columns that were not actually needed in the query.

Exceptions:

If there is no obvious, clear, simple name for the table correlation name, then use an invented name, such as a single letter like X. Likewise, if a computation has no immediate name, then you might use an invented name.

1.2.7 Relationship Table Names Should Be Common Descriptive Terms

Rationale:

Tables and views can model relationships, usually one-to-many or many-to-many, as well as entities. If the relationship has a common name that is understood in the context, then use it. There is a tendency for newbies to concatenate the names of the tables involved to build a nounce word. For example, they name a table "Marriages" because that is the common term for that relationship rather than "ManWoman," "HusbandsWives," or something really weird. Likewise, "Enrollment" makes more sense than "Students_Courses"; once you start looking for the names, they come easily.

This concatenation falls apart when the relationship is not a simple binary one, such as an escrow on a house that has a buyer, a seller, and a lender.

Exceptions:

If there is no common term for the relationship, you will need to invent something, and it might well be a concatenation of table names.

1.2.8 Metadata Schema Access Objects Can Have Names That Include Structure Information

This rule does not apply to the schema information tables, which come with standardized names. It is meant for naming indexes and other things that deal directly with storage and access. The postfix "_idx" is acceptable.

Rationale:
This is simply following the principle that a name should tell you what something is. In the case of indexes and other things that deal directly with storage and access, that is what they are. They have nothing to do with the data model.

Exceptions:
This does not apply to schema objects that are seen by the user. Look for the rules for the other schema objects as we go along.

1.3 Problems in Naming Data Elements

Now that we have talked about how to do it right, let's spend some time on common errors in names that violate the rules we set up.

1.3.1 Avoid Vague Names

Rationale:

> *"That sounds vaguely obscene to me! I can't stand vagueness!"*
> —Groucho Marx.

At one extreme the name is so general that it tells us nothing. The column is a reserved word such as "date" or it is a general word like "id," "amount," "date," and so forth. Given a column called "date," you have to ask, "date of what?" An appointment? Birth? Hire? Termination? Death? The name begs the question on the face of it.

At another extreme, the name is made useless by telling us a string of qualifiers that contradict each other. Consider the typical newbie column name like "type_code_id" as an example. If it is an identifier, then it is unique for every entity that has it, like the vehicle identification number (VIN) on a automobile. If it is a code, then what is the trusted source that maintains it like a ZIP code? It is drawn from a domain of values that is not unique. If it is a type, then what is the taxonomy to which it belongs? Why not go all the way and call it "type_code_id_value" instead?

Why did we not find a mere "customer_type" that would have been understood on sight?

Exceptions:
None

Improperly formed data element names seem to be the result of ignorance and object-oriented (OO) programming. In particular, OO programmers put "_id" on every primary key in every table and have problems understanding that SQL is a strongly typed language in which things do not change their data types in programs. The names get absurd at times. Consider a lookup table for colors:

```
CREATE TABLE TblColors
(color_value_id INTEGER NOT NULL PRIMARY KEY,
 color_value VARCHAR(50) NOT NULL);
```

But what does "_value_id" mean? Names like this are generated without thought or research. Assume that we are using the Pantone color system in the database, so we have a trusted source and a precise description—we did the research! This might have been written as follows:

```
CREATE TABLE Colors
(pantone_nbr INTEGER NOT NULL PRIMARY KEY,
 color_description VARCHAR(50) NOT NULL);
```

1.3.2 Avoid Names That Change from Place to Place

Rationale:
The worst possible design flaw is changing the name of an attribute on the fly, from table to table. As an example, consider this slightly cleaned-up piece of actual code from a SQL newsgroup:

```
SELECT Incident.Type, IPC.DefendantType,
Recommendation.Notes, Offence.StartDate, Offence.EndDate,
Offence.ReportedDateTime, IPC.URN
FROM IPC INNER JOIN Incident
ON IPC.URN = Incident.IPCURN
```

```
INNER JOIN IncidentOffence
ON Incident.URN = IncidentOffence.IncidentURN
INNER JOIN Offence
ON Offence.URN = IncidentOffence.OffenceURN
INNER JOIN IPCRecommendation
 ON IPC.URN = IPCRecommendation.IPCURN
INNER JOIN Recommendation
 ON IPCRecommendation.RecommendationID = Recommendation.ID;
```

Those full table names are difficult to read, but the newbie who wrote this code thinks that the table name must *always* be part of the column name. That is the way that a file worked in early COBOL programs.

This means that if you have hundreds of tables, each appearance of the same attribute gets a new name, so you can never build a proper data dictionary. Did you also notice that it is not easy to see underscores, commas, and periods?

Try this cleaned-up version, which clearly shows a simple star schema centered on the IPC table.

```
SELECT I1.incident_type, IPC.defendant_type, R1.notes,
       O1.start_date, O1.end_date, O1.reported_datetime, IPC.urn
  FROM Incidents AS I1, IPC, Recommendations AS R1, Offences AS O1,
 WHERE IPC.recommendation_id = R1.recommendation_id
   AND IPC.urn = O1.urn
   AND IPC.urn = I1.urn
   AND IPC.urn = R1.urn
   AND I1.urn = O1.urn;
```

I have no idea what a URN is, but it looks like a standard identifier of some kind. Look at all of the kinds of "URNs" (i.e., URN, IPCURN, and OffenseURN) in the original version of the query. It gives you the feeling of being in a crematorium gift shop.

As you walk from room to room in your house, do you also change your name, based on your physical location? Of course not! The name we seek identifies the entity, not the location.

Exceptions:

Aliases inside a query can temporarily give a new name to an occurrence of a data element. These are temporary and disappear at the end of the statement. We discuss rules for this in another section 1.2.6.

1.3.3 Do Not Use Proprietary Exposed Physical Locators

Rationale:

The most basic idea of modern data modeling is to separate the logical model and the physical implementation from each other. This allows us to reuse the model on different platforms and not be tied to just one platform.

In the old days, the logical and physical implementations were fused together. I will explain this in more detail in the next chapter, but for now the rule is to never use proprietary physical locators. We want to have portable code. But the real problem is that the proprietary physical locator violates the basic idea of a key in the relational model.

When new SQL programmers use IDENTITY, GUID, ROWID, or other auto-numbering vendor extensions to get a key that can be used for locating a given row, they are imitating a magnetic tape's sequential access. It lets them know the order in which a row was added to the table—just like individual records went onto the end of the magnetic tape!

We will spend more time discussing this flaw in Chapter 3.

Exceptions:

You might want to fake a sequential file when you are using a SQL table structure for some purpose other than a relational database management system (RDBMS). For example, staging and scrubbing data outside the "Real Schema" that do not have any data integrity issues.

Fonts, Punctuation, and Spacing

CODE IS USUALLY set in a monospace font. After more than a century of manual typewriters and decades of punchcards, we find that it is actually easier to read code in a monospace font than a proportional font. Punctuation marks get the same spacing as a letter in a monospace font, but would be lost in a proportional font.

2.1 Typography and Code

Your brain and eyes do not follow code the same way that they follow text, process mathematics, read maps, or look at pictures. In fact, there are a lot of individual differences in human brains.

Some people like text editors that use colors for various syntax elements in a programming language. Other people get headaches from colored program editors and want to see black-and-white text. Likewise, a newspaper that put nouns in red, verbs in green, and other such things would simply not work. Yet black-and-white maps are much more difficult to read than those with colors. Why? This has to do with color perception and how fast you can switch between the left and right halves of your brain.

There is a test for brain damage in which the examiner flashes cards with words printed in various colored inks (e.g., the word "RED" written in green ink). The examiner asks the subject for the word or

the color and times the responses. The rate is fairly constant over the subject's lifetime, so a change is a symptom of some physical or chemical change. Now, try reading this phrase:

Paris
in the
the Spring.

Almost nobody reading this for the first time catches the fact that the word "the" appears twice. The point is that there is a vertical component to how we read text in chunks of words.

Code on a page is read from left to right and from top to bottom, with a lot of vertical eye movement that you would not have if you were reading pure text.

A few years ago, the following posting made the rounds in newsgroups. I am not sure if it is genuinely from Cambridge University, but it makes its point very nicely:

> Aoccrdnig to rscheearch at Cmabrigde Uinervtisy, it deosn't mttaer in waht oredr the ltteers in a wrod are, the only iprmoetnt tihng is taht the frist and lsat ltteer be at the rghit pclae. The rset can be a total mses and you can sitll raed it wouthit porbelm. Tihs is bcuseae the huamn mnid does not raed ervey lteter by istlef, but the wrod as a wlohe.

Because the parser guarantees that running code will not have syntax and spelling errors like those in the above text, the reader knows what token to expect next with far more certainty than in plain text. Not only are words seen as wholes, but they are also anticipated within each statement in the programming language. That is, if I see an "IF" token in Pascal or another member of the Algol family, I anticipate the matching "THEN" that completes the statement.

Let's discuss some basic typographic conventions for programming code, which are based on how people read it.

2.1.1 Use Only Upper- and Lowercase Letters, Digits, and Underscores for Names

Rationale:

This subset of characters will port to any other programming language. It is very handy to be able to use the same names in both the database and the host languages of the applications.

For example, the octothrope or number sign (#) is allowed in several SQL products, but it has a special meaning in other programming languages and could not be used in them.

Exceptions:

If you are still programming on a machine that uses punchcards, then you have no choice but to use the limited, uppercase-only character. It is hard to imagine such a situation in the 21st century.

If the SQL implementation requires special symbols for certain names, then you have no choice. For example, temporary table names begin with an octothrope and parameter names begin with a "petite snail" or "at sign" (@) in Sybase/SQL Server T-SQL dialects. However, it is a good idea to be sure that the names are unique without the special characters, so you can port the code to a more modern implementation.

Do not use an underscore as the first or last letter in a name. It looks like the name is missing another component. Leading or trailing underscores also get lost visually without letters or digits around them, thanks to laser-quality printers. Likewise, do not use more than one underscore in a row. The old mechanical line printers could not align underscores, so you could eyeball them, whereas laser printers are microscopically precise.

2.1.2 Lowercase Scalars Such as Column Names, Parameters, and Variables

Rationale:

Words in books and newspapers are written in lowercase letters because they are easier to read than uppercase words. This is basic typography. Using all uppercase letters is the worst choice. Lowercase text is also read faster than uppercase text. The first measurements are in Woodworth (1938), and Smith and Fisher (1975) have confirmed it. Participants were asked to read comparable passages of text, half completely in uppercase text and half presented in standard lowercase text. In each study, participants read reliably faster with the lowercase text by a 5 percent to 10 percent speed difference.

Exceptions:
Unless there is a compelling physical reason, use lowercase. The only compelling physical reason I can think of is that you are still using punchcards in the 21st century.

2.1.3 Capitalize Schema Object Names

Rationale:
Schema objects include tables, views, stored procedures, and so forth. Capitalized words begin a sentence in languages that use the Latin alphabet. Additionally, capitalization represents proper nouns—like the names of sets being modeled by tables in SQL—in English, German, and other natural languages. This is the way that readers expect to see these names; don't surprise them.

Exceptions:
Unless the name naturally begins with a lowercase letter, there is no reason not to capitalize it.

2.1.4 Uppercase the Reserved Words

Rationale:
Uppercase words are seen as a unit, rather than being read as a series of syllables or letters. The eye is drawn to them, and they act to announce a statement or clause. That is why headlines and warning signs work.

Typographers use the term *bouma* for the shape of a word. The term appears in Paul Saenger's book (1975). Imagine each letter on a rectangular card that just fits it, so you see the ascenders, descenders, and baseline letters as various-sized "Lego blocks" that are snapped together to make a word.

The bouma of an uppercase word is always a simple, dense rectangle, and it is easy to pick out of a field of lowercase words. Consider this statement:

```
Select a, b, c from foobar where flob = 23;
```

versus:

```
SELECT a, b, c FROM Foobar WHERE flob = 23;
```

See how quickly you can find each clause, reading from left to right? Next, if you put each clause on a line of its own, you can read the code still faster:

```
SELECT a, b, c
  FROM Foobar
 WHERE flob = 23;
```

We will deal with rules for the vertical components later.

Exceptions:
None

Keywords come in two types, reserved and nonreserved words. The reserved words are part of the SQL language; the nonreserved words are metadata names that appear in the environment and will not cause syntax errors in an actual SQL program. They are also not very likely to be used in a real application.

```
<key word> ::= <reserved word> | <non-reserved word>

<non-reserved word> ::=
  ADA
 | C | CATALOG_NAME | CHARACTER_SET_CATALOG | CHARACTER_SET_NAME
 | CHARACTER_SET_SCHEMA | CLASS_ORIGIN | COBOL |
COLLATION_CATALOG
 | COLLATION_NAME | COLLATION_SCHEMA | COLUMN_NAME |
COMMAND_FUNCTION
 | COMMITTED
 | CONDITION_NUMBER | CONNECTION_NAME | CONSTRAINT_CATALOG
 | CONSTRAINT_NAME
 | CONSTRAINT_SCHEMA | CURSOR_NAME
 | DATA | DATETIME_INTERVAL_CODE
 | DATETIME_INTERVAL_PRECISION | DYNAMIC_FUNCTION
 | FORTRAN
 | LENGTH
 | MESSAGE_LENGTH | MESSAGE_OCTET_LENGTH | MESSAGE_TEXT | MORE |
MUMPS
 | NAME | NULLABLE | NUMBER
 | PASCAL | PLI
 | REPEATABLE | RETURNED_LENGTH | RETURNED_OCTET_LENGTH
 | RETURNED_SQLSTATE
```

```
 | ROW_COUNT
 | SCALE | SCHEMA_NAME | SERIALIZABLE | SERVER_NAME |
SUBCLASS_ORIGIN
 | TABLE_NAME | TYPE
 | UNCOMMITTED | UNNAMED

<reserved word> ::=
  ABSOLUTE | ACTION | ADD | ALL | ALLOCATE | ALTER | AND
 | ANY | ARE | AS | ASC
 | ASSERTION | AT | AUTHORIZATION | AVG
 | BEGIN | BETWEEN | BIT | BIT_LENGTH | BOTH | BY
 | CASCADE | CASCADED | CASE | CAST | CATALOG | CHAR | CHARACTER
 | CHAR_LENGTH
 | CHARACTER_LENGTH | CHECK | CLOSE | COALESCE | COLLATE |
COLLATION
 | COLUMN | COMMIT | CONNECT | CONNECTION | CONSTRAINT
 | CONSTRAINTS | CONTINUE
 | CONVERT | CORRESPONDING | COUNT | CREATE | CROSS | CURRENT
 | CURRENT_DATE | CURRENT_TIME | CURRENT_TIMESTAMP |
CURRENT_USER
 | CURSOR
 | DATE | DAY | DEALLOCATE | DEC | DECIMAL | DECLARE | DEFAULT
 | DEFERRABLE
 | DEFERRED | DELETE | DESC | DESCRIBE | DESCRIPTOR | DIAGNOSTICS
 | DISCONNECT | DISTINCT | DOMAIN | DOUBLE | DROP
 | ELSE | END | END-EXEC | ESCAPE | EXCEPT | EXCEPTION
 | EXEC | EXECUTE | EXISTS
 | EXTERNAL | EXTRACT
 | FALSE | FETCH | FIRST | FLOAT | FOR | FOREIGN | FOUND | FROM
| FULL
 | GET | GLOBAL | GO | GOTO | GRANT | GROUP
 | HAVING | HOUR
 | IDENTITY | IMMEDIATE | IN | INDICATOR | INITIALLY | INNER |
INPUT
 | INSENSITIVE | INSERT | INT | INTEGER | INTERSECT | INTERVAL |
INTO
 | IS
 | ISOLATION
 | JOIN
 | KEY
 | LANGUAGE | LAST | LEADING | LEFT | LEVEL | LIKE | LOCAL |
LOWER
```

```
  | MATCH | MAX | MIN | MINUTE | MODULE | MONTH
  | NAMES | NATIONAL | NATURAL | NCHAR | NEXT | NO | NOT | NULL
  | NULLIF | NUMERIC
  | OCTET_LENGTH | OF | ON | ONLY | OPEN | OPTION | OR
  | ORDER | OUTER
  | OUTPUT | OVERLAPS
  | PAD | PARTIAL | POSITION | PRECISION | PREPARE | PRESERVE |
PRIMARY
  | PRIOR | PRIVILEGES | PROCEDURE | PUBLIC
  | READ | REAL | REFERENCES | RELATIVE | RESTRICT | REVOKE |
RIGHT
  | ROLLBACK | ROWS
  | SCHEMA | SCROLL | SECOND | SECTION | SELECT | SESSION
  | SESSION_USER | SET
  | SIZE | SMALLINT | SOME | SPACE | SQL | SQLCODE | SQLERROR |
SQLSTATE
  | SUBSTRING | SUM | SYSTEM_USER
  | TABLE | TEMPORARY | THEN | TIME | TIMESTAMP | TIMEZONE_HOUR
  | TIMEZONE_MINUTE
  | TO | TRAILING | TRANSACTION | TRANSLATE | TRANSLATION | TRIM
 | TRUE
  | UNION | UNIQUE | UNKNOWN | UPDATE | UPPER | USAGE | USER |
USING
  | VALUE | VALUES | VARCHAR | VARYING | VIEW
  | WHEN | WHENEVER | WHERE | WITH | WORK | WRITE
  | YEAR
  | ZONE
```

Vendors will also have proprietary reserved words, which should also be capitalized.

2.1.5 Avoid the Use of CamelCase

Rationale:

The eye tends to look for a word in its usual lowercase or capitalized form, so CamelCase words tend to lead the eye to the pieces rather than to the whole word. In particular, a CamelCase word that begins with a lowercase letter will be scanned starting at the first uppercase letter and then scanned backward to get the first syllable.

Another problem is that you need to agree on how to mix the cases. For example, should it be “upcCode,” “UpcCode,” “UPCcode,” or

"UPCCode"? In practice, you can wind up with several versions of the same name.

It is even more difficult to read text in alternating case; that is, where the letters of a word change from uppercase to lowercase multiple times within a word (e.g., "AlTeRnAtInG cAsE"). The bouma shape is different from the same word in its lowercase form. Alternating case has been shown to be more difficult than either lowercase or uppercase text in a variety of studies.

Smith (1969) showed that it slowed the reading speed of a passage of text. Mason (1978) showed that the time to name a word was slowed.

Pollatsek, Well, and Schindler (1975) showed that word matching was hindered. Meyer and Gutschera (1975) showed that category decision times decreased.

Exceptions:
If the word naturally appears in CamelCase, such as "MacDonald," then use it. If you begin the object name with an uppercase letter, then you can optionally use it. However, never use CamelCase for a scalar.

2.2 Word Spacing

Put one space between language tokens and do not jam things into a stream. For example, do write "foobar = 21" instead of "foobar=21," as you will often see. Many programmers who grew up with punchcards were taught to use minimal white space to save the limited number of columns. For example, FORTRAN II does not need any spaces at all in its code, nor does the original IBM job control language (JCL) for the IBM/360 family. Modern programming languages are not this restricted, and we now have the ability to write code as if people were more important than computers.

Rationale:
We are now living in the 21st century, and you can add white space for readability without running over the edge. That is a screen and not a punchcard in front of you.

Exceptions:
You might have to wrap exceptionally long lines. This is not as big a problem in a concise language like SQL as it was in a verbose language like COBOL.

2.3 Follow Normal Punctuation Rules

Rationale:

Try to follow the rules that you would for English punctuation, because people are used to reading English and their eyes expect certain conventions.

1. In SQL in particular, you need to follow the rule about having a space after a comma because the comma and the period are easy to confuse or to miss visually.

   Compare:

   ```
   SELECT flobs.a,flobs.b,flobs.c,fleq.d
   FROM Flobs,Foobar,Fleq;
   ```

   versus

   ```
   SELECT flobs.a, flobs.b, flobs.c, fleq.d
   FROM Flobs, Foobar, Fleq;
   ```

2. Put commas at the end of a line, not the start. A comma, semicolon, question mark, or periods are visual signals that something has just ended, not that it is starting. Having a comma at the start of a line will make the eye tick leftward as it looks for that missing word that was expected before the comma.

   ```
   SELECT flobs.a
         ,flobs.b
         ,flobs.c
         ,fleq.d
     FROM Flobs
         ,Fleq
    ;
   ```

   Instead, put comma-separated lists on one line so they can be read left to right instead of vertically. If you split the list into two or more lines, see that each line contains related data elements.

   ```
   SELECT flobs.a, flobs.b, flobs.c, --related group
          fleq.d
     FROM Flobs, Fleq;
   ```

3. Put a new line or at least a space after a semicolon to separate statements.
4. Put a space between words even when you could crowd them together.

Exceptions:
If SQL does not work the same way as English, then you have to follow the SQL syntax rules.

Many of the code-formatting habits people have go back to habits they were taught by programmers who grew up with punchcard data processing. Because we have video terminals and text editors today, a lot of habits no longer have any basis.

The practice of putting a comma in front of a single variable on a single line goes back to punchcards. It was often difficult for programmers to get to a keypunch machine to create their decks of cards. In this format, you could pull or insert a card to change your code. There is no excuse for this practice since we now have video terminals.

English and European languages are read left to right and then top to bottom. This scanning pattern is so deeply learned that we arrange schematics, comic books, maps, and other graphics the same way. To see how much changing that order can throw you off, try to read a Japanese or Chinese comic book. The panels are in right-to-left order, and the Chinese word balloons are read top to bottom. This is why typographers have a rule that you do not set long words

V
E
R
T
T
I
C
A
L
L
Y.

Did you spot the misspelling? About one-third of readers do not. Likewise, it is difficult to locate duplicates and errors in those long vertical lists of names. SQL formatting can use vertical alignment to advantage in other places but in things that should be chunked together.

2.4 Use Full Reserved Words

Rational:
SQL allows you to skip some reserved words and to abbreviate others. Try to use the full forms to document the program. This is a good thing in COBOL, and it works in SQL as well.

For example, an alias can be written with or without an AS operator. That is, "Personnel AS P1" is equivalent to "Personnel P1" in a FROM clause, and "(salary + commission) AS total_pay" is equivalent to "(salary + commission) total_pay" in a SELECT list. But the AS reserved word makes it easier to see there is an alias and not a comma in these situations.

Technically, you can abbreviate INTEGER to INT and DECIMAL to DEC, but the full names are preferred. The abbreviations look like the reserved word "into" or the month "Dec" in English.

Exceptions:
The exception is to use the shorter forms of the character data types. That is, CHAR(n) instead of CHARACTER(n), VARCHAR(n) instead of VARYING CHARACTER(n), NCHAR(n) instead of NATIONAL CHARACTER(n), and NVARCHAR(n) instead of NATIONAL VARYING CHARACTER(n). The full names are too long to be comfortable to a reader. Even COBOL, the most verbose programming language on earth, allows some abbreviations.

2.5 Avoid Proprietary Reserved Words if a Standard Keyword Is Available in Your SQL Product

Rationale:
Sticking to standards will make your code readable to other SQL programmers who might not know your dialect. It also means that your code can run on other products without being rewritten.

Standard code will protect you from failure when the proprietary syntax is dropped or modified. That unwelcome surprise occurred in several products when the vendors added the Standard SQL versions of OUTER JOINs and deprecated their old proprietary versions. In particular, SQL Server programmers had to unlearn their *= syntax and semantics for outer joins.

The other disadvantage of proprietary features is that they change over time and have no standard behavior. For example, the BIT data type in SQL Server changed its NULL-ability between product releases. Oracle could not tell an empty string from a NULL. There are lots of other examples. Because there is no external standard to appeal, a vendor is free to do anything it wishes.

Exceptions:
If your SQL product does not yet support standard syntax for something, then you have no choice. This is true for temporal functions. They were late getting to Standard SQL, so the early vendors made up their own syntax and internal temporal models.

2.6 Avoid Proprietary Statements if a Standard Statement Is Available

Rationale:
This rule ought to be obvious. Sticking to standards will make your code readable to other SQL programmers who might not know your dialect. It also means that your code can run on other products without being rewritten. Standard code will protect your code from failure when the proprietary syntax is dropped or modified.

In fact, a vendor can actually give you proprietary features that are unpredictable! In the "Books On Line" interactive manual that comes with Microsoft SQL Server, we get a warning in the REMARKS section about the proprietary "UPDATE.. FROM.." syntax that tells us:

> The results of an UPDATE statement are undefined if the statement includes a FROM clause that is not specified in such a way that only one value is available for each column occurrence that is updated (in other words, if the UPDATE statement is not deterministic). For example, given the UPDATE statement in the following script, both rows in table S meet the qualifications of the FROM clause in the UPDATE statement, but it is undefined which row from S is used to update the row in table T.

This replaces a prior behavior found in the Sybase and Ingres family where the UPDATE.. FROM would do multiple updates, one for each joined row in the second table.

In older versions of Sybase/SQL Server, if a base table row is represented more than once in the embedded query, then that row is operated on multiple times instead of just once. This is a total violation of relational principles, but it's easy to do with the underlying physical implementation. Here is a quick example:

```
CREATE TABLE T1 (x INTEGER NOT NULL);
INSERT INTO T1 VALUES (1);
INSERT INTO T1 VALUES (2);
INSERT INTO T1 VALUES (3);
INSERT INTO T1 VALUES (4);

CREATE TABLE T2 (x INTEGER NOT NULL);
INSERT INTO T2 VALUES (1);
INSERT INTO T2 VALUES (1);
INSERT INTO T2 VALUES (1);
INSERT INTO T2 VALUES (1);
```

Now try to update T1 by doubling all the rows that have a match in T2.

```
UPDATE  T1
   SET T1.x = 2 * T1.x
  FROM T2
 WHERE T1.x = T2.x;

SELECT * FROM T1;


original   current
    x          x
  ====       ====
   16          2
    2          2
    3          3
    4          4
```

The FROM clause gives you a CROSS JOIN, so you get a series of four actions on the same row (1 => 2 => 4 => 8 => 16). These are pretty simple examples, but you get the idea. There are subtle things with self-joins and the diseased mutant T-SQL syntax that can hang you in loops

by changing things, or you can have tables that depend on the order of the rows for their results, and so forth.

SQL Server and Sybase used different fixes for this problem in later versions of their products. Sybase did a hidden "SELECT DISTINCT" in the implied query, and SQL Server gets an unpredictable row. Standard SQL is consistent and clear about aliases, views, and derived tables, as well as a highly orthogonal language.

If the UPDATE clause could take an alias, according to the Standard SQL model, then you would create a copy of the contents of that base table under the alias name, then update that copy, and delete it when the statement was over—in effect doing nothing to the base table.

If the UPDATE clause could take a FROM clause, according to the Standard SQL model, then you would create a result set from the table expression, then update that copy, and delete it when the statement was over—in effect doing nothing to the base tables.

Because this syntax is so proprietary, inconsistent with the standard model, and ambiguous, why does it exist? In the original Sybase product, the physical model made this "extension" relatively easy to implement, and there were no standards or a good understanding of the relational model back then. Programmers got used to it and then it was almost impossible to fix.

When I lived in Indianapolis in the mid-1970s, my neighbor had graduated from General Motors private college and gone to work for the company. His first job was investigating industrial accident reports. We were having a beer one night, and he got to telling war stories from the various General Motors plants he had been to for his job. His conclusion after a year on that job was that all industrial accidents are bizarre suicide attempts. People would go to the machine shop and build clever devices to short around the safety features on their equipment so they could work a little faster.

For example, if you make a clamp that holds in one of the two safety switches that operates a small stamping machine, you can push the other button with one hand and work material with your free hand. Well, you can do this until that free hand is crushed just above the wrist and squirts across the back wall of the shop anyway. Trading speed for safety and correctness will eventually catch up with you.

Exceptions:

If your SQL product does not yet support standard syntax for something, then you have no choice. For example, Oracle did not support the CASE expression, but its DECODE() function is quite close to it and can be substituted in older versions of Oracle.

2.7 Rivers and Vertical Spacing

When you look at a magazine or newspaper, you will notice that the text is set in a column that is even on both sides. This is called justified text, as opposed to ragged right or ragged left text. Extra spacing is added to each line to justify the text, but if this extra spacing appears in the same location on several rows, you get rivers.

A *river* is a vertical open space in text, and it is considered to be bad typography. You want to read text from left to right, top to bottom, with a visual break at the indentation or new line that marks the start of a paragraph. A river pulls your eye downward and makes the text more difficult to read.

It is easy to set up what typographers call rivers in the program code in a monospace font because you can add spacing as needed, but that same downward river effect aligns code on a vertical axis and makes the program easier to read.

```
SELECT I1.incident_type, IPC.defendant_type, R1.notes,
O1.start_date, O1.end_date, O1.reported_datetime, IPC.urn
FROM Incidents AS I1, IPC, Recommendations AS R1, Offences AS
O1,
WHERE IPC.recommendation_id = R1.recommendation_id
AND IPC.urn = O1.urn AND IPC.urn = I1.urn
AND IPC.urn = R1.urn AND I1.urn = O1.urn;
```

versus no river:

```
SELECT I1.incident_type, IPC.defendant_type, R1.notes,
       O1.start_date, O1.end_date, O1.reported_datetime, IPC.urn
  FROM Incidents AS I1, IPC, Recommendations AS R1, Offences AS
O1,
 WHERE IPC.recommendation_id = R1.recommendation_id
   AND IPC.urn = O1.urn
   AND IPC.urn = I1.urn
   AND IPC.urn = R1.urn
   AND I1.urn = O1.urn;
```

2.8 Indentation

When you have to indent in block-structured 3GL programming languages, use three spaces. A single space is too short to be read as anything but a word separator. Two spaces will work because that is what you were probably taught to use in typing classes at the end of a sentence, but three spaces or a new line is clearly a paragraph to the reader.

Indenting five or more spaces actually hurts readability. The eye has to skip over too far to grab the code. In particular, the use of an eight-space tab character is historical. The early Teletype machines had 80 characters per line and set tabs at eight spaces for mechanical reasons. That became the definition when we moved to electronic terminals.

The rule for SQL is that rivers override what we were doing in the old 3GL languages.

Rationale:

What we need in data manipulation language (DML) is a balance of indentation and the use of rivers to the logical nesting. Note how each subquery has a river to hold it together and that the subquery is placed against the river.

```
SELECT DISTINCT pilot
  FROM PilotSkills AS PS1
 WHERE NOT EXISTS
       (SELECT *
          FROM Hangar
         WHERE NOT EXISTS
               (SELECT *
                  FROM PilotSkills AS PS2
                 WHERE PS1.pilot = PS2.pilot
                   AND PS2.plane = Hangar.plane));
```

Exceptions:

A subquery is always inside parentheses, so one can make a case that the closing parentheses should align vertically with its mate.

```
SELECT DISTINCT pilot
  FROM PilotSkills AS PS1
 WHERE NOT EXISTS
       (SELECT *
```

```
    FROM Hangar
   WHERE NOT EXISTS
         (SELECT *
            FROM PilotSkills AS PS2
           WHERE PS1.pilot = PS2.pilot
             AND PS2.plane = Hangar.plane
         )
 );
```

The advantage is that you can quickly find the limits of the subquery but at the cost of extra lines that hold only one or two tokens.

When you have a group of related columns in the SELECT clause list or other places, then use the three-space rule to indent the members of the group when you have to go to a second line:

```
SELECT C1.cust_name, C1.street_address, C1.city, C1.state,
C1.zip,
       P1.payment_1, P1.payment_2, P1.payment_3, P1.payment_4,
         P1.payment_5, P1.payment_6, P1.payment_7, P1.payment_8,
          P1.payment_9, payment_10,
  FROM Customers AS C1, Payments AS P1
 WHERE C1.cust_id = P1.cust_id;
```

The customer columns are on one line, while the 10 payments are split over three lines with an indentation to group them.

2.9 Use Line Spacing to Group Statements

Rationale:

Use one new line between related statements and two new lines between separate steps in the same process.

Clusters of related code on a page show the reader which statements perform each step of a process. It is also a good idea to introduce each step with a high-level comment, but we will get into that later.

As an experiment to demonstrate how important visual clustering is, make some flash cards with some red circles on them. On one set of flash cards, arrange the spots in the patterns in which they appear on a double nine set of dominoes. On a second set of flash cards, put the spots on at random.

Show the cards to your subjects for one second each and call out the number of the card. Ask them to write down the number of spots on

each card. When there is no arrangement, most people start having problems at five spots and almost nobody can handle eight or more randomly arranged cards. However, nine spots in a three-by-three arrangement present no problems. Even the 10 spots on a playing card are easy to count because they are broken into two clusters of five spots.

Exceptions:

The double spacing between steps can be optional if it breaks up the flow of the code.

Data Declaration Language

"[I need] Data! Data! Data! I can't make bricks without clay."
—Sherlock Holmes
(fictional detective of author Sir Arthur Conan Doyle)

"Smart data structures and dumb code works a lot better than the other way round."
—Eric S. Raymond

I BELIEVE THAT MOST of the bad SQL queries in the world are the result of bad schema design. A bad schema can be ambiguous, require extra work to fetch data, and not return valid results even when good data was input into it.

Let's start with the syntax rules that should be followed when writing data declaration language (DDL), and then in the following chapters, talk about the content and semantics of the DDL.

3.1 Put the Default in the Right Place

Rationale:
The DEFAULT constraint appears after the data type and NOT NULL constraint appears after the DEFAULT value.

The SQL-92 standard requires that ordering, but most products allow you to place the DEFAULT either after the data type or after the

NOT NULL constraint. A NULL-able column can also have a DEFAULT value, so the standard makes sense. Because we need a consistent pattern, let's go with the standard. Because NOT NULL is so common, it can be left on the same line as the DEFAULT and data type.

Exceptions:
None

3.2 The Default Value Should Be the Same Data Type as the Column

Rationale:
That rule sounds obvious, but programmers do not follow it. You will see columns with decimal places defaulted to integer zero, columns of CHAR (n) defaulted to strings of less than (n) characters, and columns of TIMESTAMP defaulted to DATE. The result in many SQL products was implicit type conversions whenever a default value was used. Why incur that overhead, when you could get it right in the first place?

Exceptions:
None

3.3 Do Not Use Proprietary Data Types

Rationale:
Proprietary data types do not port to other products or from one release to another of the same product. Standard SQL has more than enough data types to model most of the things you will find in the real world.

As an example, only the SQL Server/Sybase family has a MONEY data type. It adds currency symbols and commas to a numeric string for display, but it has different rules for doing computations than NUMERIC or DECIMAL data types. The front end has to handle the currency symbols and commas and be sure that the basic math is correct. Why do something in the DDL only to undo it in the front end?

Even worse, machine-level things like a BIT or BYTE data type have no place in a high-level language like SQL. SQL is a high-level language; it is abstract and defined without regard to physical implementation. This basic principle of data modeling is called *data abstraction*.

Bits and bytes are the lowest units of hardware-specific, physical implementation you can get. Are you on a high-end or low-end machine? Does the machine have 8-, 16-, 32-, 64-, or 128-bit words? Twos complement or ones complement math? Hey, the standards allow decimal-based machines, so bits do not exist at all! What about NULLs? To be a data type, you have to have NULLs, so what is a NULL bit? By definition, a bit is on or off and has no NULL.

What does the implementation of the host languages do with bits? Did you know that +1, +0, -0, and -1 are all used for Booleans but not consistently? That means all of the host languages—present, future, and not yet defined. Surely no good programmer would ever write nonportable code by getting to such a low level as bit fiddling!

You might also ask if zero is used for "successful completion" in the functions of the host language or the vendor's own 4GL. There are two situations in practice. Either the bits are individual attributes or they are used as a vector to represent a single attribute. In the case of a single attribute, the encoding is limited to two values, which do not port to host languages or other SQLs, cannot be easily understood by an end user, and cannot be expanded.

In the second case, what some newbies, who are still thinking in terms of second- and third-generation programming languages or even punchcards, do is build a vector for a series of yes/no status codes, failing to see the status vector as a single attribute. Did you ever play the children's game "20 Questions" when you were young?

Imagine you have six components for a loan approval, so you allocate bits in your second-generation model of the world. You have 64 possible vectors, but only 5 of them are valid (i.e., you cannot be rejected for bankruptcy and still have good credit). For your data integrity, you can:

1. Ignore the problem. This is actually what most newbies do. When the database becomes a mess without any data integrity, they move on to the second solution.

2. Write elaborate ad hoc CHECK() constraints with user-defined functions or proprietary bit-level library functions that cannot port and that run like cold glue.

Now we add a seventh condition to the vector: Which end does it go on? Why? How did you get it in the right place on all the possible hardware that it will ever use? Did the code that references a bit in a word by its position do it right after the change?

You need to sit down and think about how to design an encoding of the data that is high level, general enough to expand, abstract, and portable. For example, is that loan approval a hierarchical code?

Concatenation code? Vector code? Did you provide codes for unknown, missing, and N/A values? It is not easy to design such things!

Exceptions:

Very, very special circumstances where there is no alternative at the present time might excuse the use of proprietary data types. In 20 years of consulting on SQL programming, I have never found a situation that could not be handled by a basic data type or a CREATE DOMAIN statement.

Next, consider porting a proprietary data type by building a user-defined distinct type that matches the proprietary data type. This is not always possible, so check your product. If the data type is exotic, such as Geo/Spatial data, sound, images, or documents, you should probably do the job in a specialized system and not SQL.

3.4 Place the PRIMARY KEY Declaration at the Start of the CREATE TABLE Statement

Rationale:

Having the key as the first thing you read in a table declaration gives you important information about the nature of the table and how you will find the entities in it. For example, if I have a table named "Personnel" and the first column is "ssn," I immediately know that we track employees via their Social Security numbers.

Exceptions:

In the case of a compound primary key, the columns that make up the key might not fit nicely into the next rule (3.5). If this is the case, then put a comment by each component of the primary key to make it easier to find.

3.5 Order the Columns in a Logical Sequence and Cluster Them in Logical Groups

Rationale:

The physical order of the columns within a table is not supposed to matter in the relational model. Their names and not their ordinal positions identify columns, but SQL has ordinal positions for columns in tables in default situations. The SELECT * and INSERT INTO statements use the order of declaration in their default actions.

This rule is obvious; people prefer a logical ordering of things to a random mix. For example, the columns for an address are best put in their expected order: name, street, city, state, and postal code.

Exceptions:
Thanks to columns being added after the schema is in place, you might not be able to arrange the table as you would like in your SQL product. Check to see if your product allows column reordering.

If you have a physical implementation that uses the column ordering in some special way, you need to take advantage of it. For example, DB2 for z/OS logs changes from the first byte changed to the last byte changed, unless the row is variable; then it logs from the first byte changed to the end of the row. If the change does not cause the length of the variable row to change size, it goes back to logging from the first byte changed to the last byte changed. The DBA can take advantage of this knowledge to optimize performance by placing:

- Infrequently updated nonvariable columns first
- Infrequently updated variable-length columns next
- Frequently updated columns last
- Columns that are frequently modified together next to each other

Following this approach will cause DB2 to log the least amount of data most of the time. Because the log can be a significant bottleneck for performance, this approach is handy. You can always create the table and then create a view for use by developers that resequences the columns into the logical order if it is that important.

3.6 Indent Referential Constraints and Actions under the Data Type

Rationale:
The idea is to make the full column declaration appear as one visual unit when you read down the CREATE TABLE statement. In particular, put the ON DELETE and ON UPDATE clauses on separate lines.

The standard does not require that they appear together in any particular order. As an arbitrary decision, I am going to tell you to use alphabetical order, so ON DELETE comes before ON UPDATE if both are present.

Exceptions:
None

3.7 Give Constraints Names in the Production Code

Rationale:
The constraint name will show up in error messages when it is violated. This gives you the ability to create meaningful messages and easily locate the errors.

The syntax is simply "CONSTRAINT <name>," and it should be a clear statement of what has been violated done as a name. For example:

```
CREATE TABLE Prizes
(..
 award_points INTEGER DEFAULT 0 NOT NULL
              CONSTRAINT award_point_range
              CHECK (award_points BETWEEN 0 AND 100),
 ..);
```

If you do not provide a name, the SQL engine will probably provide a machine-generated name that is very long, impossible to read, and will give you no clue about the nature of your problem.

Exceptions:
You can leave off constraint names on PRIMARY KEYS, UNIQUE, and FOREIGN KEY constraints, because most SQL products will give an explicit error message about them when they are violated. The exception is that Oracle will use the system-generated name when it displays the execution plans.

You can leave off constraint names during development work. However, remember that constraint names are global, not local, because the CREATE ASSERTION statement would have problems otherwise.

3.8 Put CHECK() Constraint Near what they Check

Rationale:
Put single column CHECK() constraints on its column, multicolumn constraints near their columns.

We want as much information about a column on that column as possible. Having to look in several places for the definition of a column can only cost us time and accuracy. Likewise, put multicolumn constraints as near to the columns involved as is reasonable.

Exceptions:
If your SQL product has a CREATE DOMAIN statement, you will include DEFAULT and CHECK() constraints in the domain declaration, so the use of the DOMAIN is enough. Multicolumn constraints on columns that are far apart should be moved to the end of the table declaration. This will give you one place to look for the more complex constraints, rather than trying to look all over the DDL statement.

It can also be argued that none of this really matters, because most of the time we should be going to the schema information tables to retrieve the constraint definitions, not the DDL. Constraints may have been removed or added with subsequent ALTER statements, and the system catalog will have the correct, current state, whereas the DDL may not.

3.8.1 Consider Range Constraints for Numeric Values

Rationale:
The whole idea of a database is that it is a single trusted repository for all of the data in the enterprise. This is the place where the business rules must be enforced.

The most common constraint on numbers in a data model is that they are not less than zero. Now look at actual DDL and see how often you find that constraint. Programmers are lazy and do not bother with this level of details.

Exceptions:
When the column really can take any value whatsoever.

3.8.2 Consider LIKE and SIMILAR TO Constraints for Character Values

Rationale:
Again, the whole idea of a database is that it is a single trusted repository for all of the data in the enterprise. This is the place where the business rules must be enforced.

An encoding will have a format that can be validated with a LIKE or SIMILAR TO predicate. Now look at actual DDL and see how often you find that constraint. This is not as portable an option as numeric range checking, and many programmers who did not use UNIX in their youth have problems with regular expressions, but it is still important.

Exceptions:
When the column really can take any value whatsoever.

3.8.3 Remember That Temporal Values Have Duration

There is no such thing as a point in time. You can ask Einstein or go back to the Greek philosopher Zeno and his famous paradoxes. Temporal values have duration, and you need to remember that they have a start and finish time, either explicitly or implicitly, that includes all of the continuum bound by them. The implicit model is a single column and the explicit model uses a pair of temporal values.

For example, when you set a due date for a payment, you usually mean any point from the start of that day up to but not including midnight of the following day. When you say an employee worked on a given date, you usually mean the event occurred during an eight-hour duration within that day.

Remember that you can use a DEFAULT CURRENT_TIMESTAMP on a temporal column and that a NULL can be used as a marker for "eternity" in the finish time column. A CHECK() constraint can round off time values to the start of the nearest year, month, day, hour, minute, or second as needed.

3.8.4 REAL and FLOAT Data Types Should Be Avoided

Most commercial applications do not need floating-point math. SQL has NUMERIC and DECIMAL data types that can be set to a great deal of scale and precision and do not have floating-point numeric rounding errors. There will be exceptions for scientific and statistical data.

3.9 Put Multiple Column Constraints as Near to Both Columns as Possible

Rationale:

Do not make the reader have to look in multiple physical locations to find all of the columns involved in the constraint. You do not have to indent this constraint, but it is a good idea to split it on two lines: one with the CONSTRAINT clause and one with the CHECK() clause.

```
CREATE TABLE Prizes
(..
 birth_date DATE NOT NULL,
 prize_date DATE NOT NULL,
 CONSTRAINT over_18_to_win
 CHECK (birth_date + INTERVAL 18 YEARS >= prize_date),
 ..);
```

Exceptions:
This is not always physically possible, especially when many columns are involved.

3.10 Put Table-Level CHECK() Constraints at the End of the Table Declaration

Rationale:
These constraints are not yet well supported in SQL products, but they are legal SQL-92 syntax. Their predicates involve the entire table as a whole rather than just single rows. This implies that they will involve aggregate functions.

```
CREATE TABLE Prizes
(..
CONSTRAINT only_5_prizes_each_winner
 CHECK (NOT EXISTS
         (SELECT *
            FROM Prizes AS P1
           GROUP BY P1.contestant_id
          HAVING COUNT(*) > 5)),
CONSTRAINT no_missing_ticket_nbrs
CHECK ((SELECT MAX(ticket_nbr) - MIN(ticket_nbr) + 1
         FROM Prizes AS P1)
       = (SELECT COUNT(ticket_nbr)
            FROM Prizes AS P1));
```

Exceptions:
None

3.11 Use CREATE ASSERTION for Multi-table Constraints

Rationale:
Put multiple table CHECK() Constraints in CREATE ASSERTION statements rather than on a table declaration.

These constraints are not yet well supported in SQL products, but they are legal SQL-92 syntax. Their predicates involve several different tables, not just one table. This implies that they are at a higher level and should be modeled there. The practical consideration is that all constraints are TRUE on an empty table, so the CREATE ASSERTION

statement lets you control that possibility. The assertion name acts as the constraint name.

```
CREATE ASSERTION enough_money_to_pay_prizes
AS
CHECK ((SELECT SUM(prize_money)
          FROM Prizes AS P1)
       <= (SELECT SUM(cash_on_hand)
             FROM Bank));
```

Exceptions:

If the SQL product does not support CREATE ASSERTION statements, then this cannot be done, but if it were possible, then violation would require a strong reason having to do with the schema design.

3.12 Keep CHECK() Constraints Single Purposed

Rationale:

Put simple CHECK() constraints in their own clauses rather than writing one long constraint with multiple tests.

When you give a constraint a name, that name will appear in error messages and can help the user to correct data. If all of the validation is in one single CHECK() clause, what name would you give it? For example, imagine a single validation for a name that looks for correct capitalization, extra spaces, and a length over five characters. About all you can call it is "bad address line" and hope the user can figure out how to fix it. However, if there were separate checks for capitalization, extra spaces, and a length over five characters, then those constraint names would be obvious and give the user a clue as to the actual problem.

Exceptions:

If your SQL product supports the SIMILAR TO predicate (a version of grep() based on the POSIX standard in Standard SQL), then you might consider having a longer regular expression with OR-ed patterns that fall under a general constraint name.

If you do not want to give details about errors to users for security reasons, then you can use a single constraint with a vague name. This would be a strange situation.

3.13 Every Table Must Have a Key to Be a Table

Rationale:

This is the very definition of a table. The problem is that many newbies do not understand what a key really is. A key must be a subset of the attributes (columns) in the table. There is no such thing as a universal, one-size-fits-all key. Just as no two sets of entities are the same, the attributes that make them unique have to be found in the reality of the data. God did not put a 17-letter Hebrew number on the bottom of everything in creation.

Here is my classification of types of keys (Table 3.1).

Table 3.1 *Types of keys*

	Natural Key	**Artificial Key**	**Exposed Locator**	**System Surrogate**
Constructed from Reality of the Data Model	Yes	No	No	No
Verifiable in Reality	Yes	No, trusted source	No	No
Validation in Itself	Yes	Yes, check digit, syntax |	No	No
Portable to New Platform	Yes	Yes	No	No
Visible to the User	Yes	Yes	Yes	No, and can be changed by engine

1. *A natural key is a subset of attributes that occurs in a table and acts as a unique identifier*. The user sees them. You can go to the external reality and verify them. You would also like to have some validation rule. Example: UPC codes on consumer goods are easily seen (read the package bar code), and you validate them with a scanner, a manual-check digit calculation, or a manufacturer's Web site.

2. *An artificial key is an extra attribute added to the table that is seen by the user*. It does not exist in the external reality but can be

verified for syntax or check digits inside itself. Example: The open codes in the UPC scheme that a user can assign to his or her own products. The check digit still works the same way, but you have to verify the codes inside your own enterprise.

If you have to construct a key yourself, it takes time to design it, to invent a validation rule, and so forth. There is a chapter on that topic in this book. Chapter 5 discusses the design of encoding schemes.

3. *An exposed physical locator is not based on attributes in the data model and is exposed to the user*. There is no way to predict it or verify it. The system obtains a value through some physical process in the storage hardware that is totally unrelated to the logical data model. Example: IDENTITY columns in the T-SQL family; other proprietary, nonrelational auto-numbering devices; and cylinder and track locations on the hard drive used in Oracle.

   Technically, these are not really keys at all, because they are attributes of the physical storage and are not even part of the logical data model, but they are handy for lazy, non-RDBMS programmers who don't want to research or think! This is the worst way to program in SQL.

4. *A surrogate key is system generated to replace the actual key behind the covers where the user never sees it*. It is based on attributes in the table. Example: Teradata hashing algorithms, pointer chains.

   The fact that you can never see or use them for DELETE and UPDATE or create them for INSERT is vital. When users can get to them, they will screw up the data integrity by getting the real keys and these physical locators out of sync. The system must maintain them.

Notice that people get exposed physical locator and surrogate mixed up; they are totally different concepts.

3.13.1 Auto-Numbers Are Not Relational Keys

In an RDBMS, the data elements exist at the schema level. You put tables together from attributes, with the help of a data dictionary to model entities in SQL.

But in a traditional 3GL-language application, the names are local to each file because each application program gives them names and meaning. Fields and subfields had to be completely specified to locate the data. There are important differences between a file system and a database, a table and a file, a row and a record, and a column and a field. If you do not have a good conceptual model, you hit a ceiling and cannot get past a certain level of competency.

In 25 words or less, it is "logical versus physical," but it goes beyond that. A file system is a loose collection of files, which have a lot of redundant data in them. A database system is a single unit that models the entire enterprise as tables, constraints, and so forth.

3.13.2 Files Are Not Tables

Files are independent of each other, whereas tables in a database are interrelated. You open an entire database, not single tables within it, but you do open individual files. An action on one file cannot affect another file unless they are in the same application program; tables can interact without your knowledge via DRI actions, triggers, and so on.

The original idea of a database was to collect data in a way that avoided redundant data in too many files and not have it depend on a particular programming language.

A file is made up of records, and records are made up of fields. A file is ordered and can be accessed by a physical location, whereas a table is not. Saying "first record," "last record," and "next *n* records" makes sense in a file, but there is no concept of a "first row," "last row," and "next row" in a table.

A file is usually associated with a particular language—ever try to read a FORTRAN file with a COBOL program? A database is language independent; the internal SQL data types are converted into host language data types.

A field exists only because of the program reading it; a column exists because it is in a table in a database. A column is independent of any host language application program that might use it.

In a procedural language, "READ a, b, c FROM FileX;" does not give the same results as "READ b, c, a FROM FileX;" and you can even write "READ a, a, a FROM FileX;" so you overwrite your local variable. In SQL, "SELECT a, b, c FROM TableX" returns the same data as "SELECT b, c, a FROM TableX" because things are located by name, not position.

A field is fixed or variable length, can repeat with an OCCURS in COBOL, struct in c, and so on. A field can change data types (union in

'C', VARIANT in Pascal, REDEFINES in COBOL, EQUIVALENCE in FORTRAN).

A column is a scalar value, drawn from a single domain (domain = data type + constraints + relationships) and represented in one and only one data type. You have no idea whatsoever how a column is physically represented internally because you never see it directly.

Consider temporal data types: in SQL Server, DATETIME (their name for TIMESTAMP data type) is a binary number internally (UNIX-style system clock representation), but TIMESTAMP is a string of digits in DB2 (COBOL-style time representation). When you have a field, you have to worry about that physical representation. SQL says not to worry about the bits; you think of data in the abstract.

Fields have no constraints, no relationships, and no data type; each application program assigns such things, and they don't have to assign the same ones! That lack of data integrity was one of the reasons for RDBMS.

Rows and columns have constraints. Records and fields can have anything in them and often do! Talk to anyone who has tried to build a data warehouse about that problem. My favorite is finding the part number "I hate my job" in a file during a data warehouse project.

Dr. Codd (1979) defined a row as a representation of a single simple fact. A record is usually a combination of a lot of facts. That is, we don't normalize a file; you stuff data into it and hope that you have everything you need for an application. When the system needs new data, you add fields to the end of the records. That is how we got records that were measured in Kbytes.

3.13.3 Look for the Properties of a Good Key

Rationale:

A checklist of desirable properties for a key is a good way to do a design inspection. There is no need to be negative all the time.

1. *Uniqueness*. The first property is that the key be unique. This is the most basic property it can have because without uniqueness it cannot be a key by definition. Uniqueness is necessary, but not sufficient.

   Uniqueness has a context. An identifier can be unique in the local database, in the enterprise across databases, or unique universally. We would prefer the last of those three options.

   We can often get universal uniqueness with industry: standard codes such as VINs. We can get enterprise uniqueness with things like telephone extensions and e-mail addresses. An identifier that is unique only in a single database is workable but pretty much useless because it will lack the other desired properties.

2. *Stability*. The second property we want is stability or invariance. The first kind of stability is within the schema, and this applies to both key and nonkey columns. The same data element should have the same representation wherever it appears in the schema. It should not be CHAR(n) in one place and INTEGER in another. The same basic set of constraints should apply to it. That is, if we use the VIN as an identifier, then we can constrain it to be only for vehicles from Ford Motors; we cannot change the format of the VIN in one table and not in all others.

   The next kind of stability is over time. You do not want keys changing frequently or in unpredictable ways. Contrary to a popular myth, this does not mean that keys cannot ever change. As the scope of their context grows, they should be able to change.

   On January 1, 2005, the United States added one more digit to the UPC bar codes used in the retail industry. The reason was globalization and erosion of American industrial domination. The global bar-code standard will be the European Article Number (EAN) Code. The American Universal Product Code (UPC) turned 30 years old in 2004 and was never so universal after all.

   The EAN was set up in 1977 and uses 13 digits, whereas the UPC has 12 digits, of which you see 10 broken into two groups of 5 digits on a label. The Uniform Code Council, which sets the standards in North America, has the details for the conversion worked out.

   More than 5 billion bar-coded products are scanned every day on earth. It has made data mining in retail possible and saved millions of hours of labor. Why would you make up your own code and stick labels on everything? Thirty years ago, consumer groups protested that shoppers would be cheated if price tags were not on each item, labor protested possible job losses, and environmentalists said that laser scanners in the bar-code readers might damage people's eyes. The neo-Luddites have been with us a long time.

For the neo-Luddite programmers who think that changing a key is going to kill you, let me quote John Metzger, chief information officer of A&P. The grocery chain had 630 stores in 2004, and the grocery industry works 1 percent to 3 percent profit margins—the smallest margins of any industry that is not taking a loss. A&P has handled the new bar-code problem as part of a modernization of its technology systems. "It is important," Mr. Metzger said, "but it is not a shut-the-company-down kind of issue."

Along the same lines, ISBN in the book trade is being changed to 13 digits, and VINs are being redesigned. See the following sources for more information:

```
(EAN: "Bar Code Détente: U.S. Finally Adds One More
Digit," July 12, 2004, New York Times, by Steve Lohr;
http://www.nytimes.com/2004/07/12/business/
12barcode.html?ex=1090648405&ei=1&en=202cb9baba72e846)
(VIN: http://www.cars.com/news/stories/
070104_storya_dn.jhtml?page=newsstory&aff=national)
(ISBN: http://www.isbn.org/standards/home/isbn/
transition.asp)
```

3. *Familiarity*. It helps if the users know something about the data. This is not quite the same as validation, but it is related. Validation can tell you if the code is properly formed via some process; familiarity can tell you if it feels right because you know something about the context. Thus, ICD codes for disease would confuse a patient but not a medical records clerk.

4. *Validation*. Can you look at the data value and tell that it is wrong, without using an external source? For example, I know that "2004-02-30" is not a valid date because no such day exists on the Common Era calendar. Check digits and fixed format codes are one way of obtaining this validation.

5. *Verifiability*. How do I verify a key? This also comes in context and in levels of trust. When I cash a check at the supermarket, the clerk is willing to believe that the photo on the driver's license I present is really me, no matter how ugly it is. Or rather, the clerk used to believe it was me; the Kroger grocery store chain is now putting an inkless fingerprinting system in place, just like many banks have done.

When I get a passport, I need a birth certificate and fingerprinting. There is a little less trust here. When I get a security clearance, I also need to be investigated. There is a lot less trust.

A key without a verification method has no data integrity and will lead to the accumulation of bad data.

6. *Simplicity*. A key should be as simple as possible, but no simpler. People, reports, and other systems will use the keys. Long, complex keys are more subject to error; storing and transmitting them is not an issue anymore, the way it was 40 or 50 years ago.

   One person's simple is another person's complex. For an example of a horribly complex code that is in common international usage, look up the International Standard Bank Number (IBAN). A country code at the start of the string determines how to parse the rest of the string, and it can be up to 34 alphanumeric characters in length. Why? Each country has its own account numbering systems, currencies, and laws, and they seldom match. In effect, the IBAN is a local banking code hidden inside an international standard (see http://www.ecbs.org/iban/iban.htm and the European Committee for Banking Standards Web site for publications).

More and more programmers who have absolutely no database training are being told to design a database. They are using GUIDs, IDENTITY, ROWID, and other proprietary auto-numbering features in SQL products to imitate either a record number (sequential file system mindset) or OID (OO mindset) because they don't know anything else. This magical, universal, one-size-fits-all numbering is totally nonrelational, depends on the physical state of the hardware at a particular time, and is a poor attempt at mimicking a magnetic tape file system.

Experienced database designers tend toward intelligent keys they find in industry-standard codes, such as UPC, VIN, GTIN, ISBN, and so on. They know that they need to verify the data against the reality they are modeling. A trusted external source is a good thing to have.

The reasons given for this poor programming practice are many, so let me go down the list:

Q: Couldn't a natural compound key become very long?
A1: So what? This is the 21st century, and we have much better computers than we did in the 1950s when key size was a real physical issue. What is funny to me is the number of idiots who replace a natural two- or three-integer compound key with a huge GUID, which no human being or other system can possibly understand, because they think it will be faster and easy to program.
A2: This is an implementation problem that the SQL engine can handle. For example, Teradata is a SQL designed for very large database (VLDB) applications that use hashing instead of B-tree or other indexes. They guarantee that no search requires more than two probes, no matter how large the database. A tree index requires more and more probes as the size of the database increases.
A3: A long key is not always a bad thing for performance. For example, if I use (city, state) as my key, I get a free index on just (city). I can also add extra columns to the key to make it a super-key when such a super-key gives me a covering index (i.e., an index that contains all of the columns required for a query, so that the base table does not have to be accessed at all).

Q: Can't I make things really fast on the current release of my SQL software?
A1: Sure, if I want to lose all of the advantages of an abstract data model, SQL set-oriented programming, carry extra data, and destroy the portability of code. Look at any of the newsgroups and see how difficult it is to move the various exposed physical locators in the same product.

The auto-numbering features are a holdover from the early SQLs, which were based on contiguous storage file systems. The data was kept in physically contiguous disk pages, in physically contiguous rows, made up of physically contiguous columns. In short, just like a deck of punchcards or a magnetic tape. Most programmers still carry that mental model, too.

But physically contiguous storage is only one way of building a relational database, and it is not the best one. The basic idea of a relational database is that the user is not supposed to know how or where things are stored at all, much less write code that depends on the particular physical representation in a particular release of a particular product on particular hardware at a particular time.

The first practical consideration is that auto-numbering is proprietary and nonportable, so you know that you will have maintenance problems when you change releases or port your system to other products. Newbies actually think they will never port code! Perhaps they only work for companies that are failing and will be gone. Perhaps their code is such a disaster that nobody else wants their application.

But let's look at the logical problems. First, try to create a table with two columns and try to make them both auto-numbered. If you cannot declare more than one column to be of a certain data type, then that thing is not a data type at all, by definition. It is a property that belongs to the physical table, not the logical data in the table.

Next, create a table with one column and make it an auto-number. Now try to insert, update, and delete different numbers from it. If you cannot insert, update, and delete rows, then it is not really a table by definition.

Finally, create a simple table with one hidden auto-number column and a few other columns. Use a few statements like:

```
INSERT INTO Foobar (a, b, c) VALUES ('a1', 'b1', 'c1');
INSERT INTO Foobar (a, b, c) VALUES ('a2', 'b2', 'c2');
INSERT INTO Foobar (a, b, c) VALUES ('a3', 'b3', 'c3');
```

Put a few rows into the table and notice that the auto-numbering feature sequentially numbered them in the order they were presented. If you delete a row, the gap in the sequence is not filled in, and the sequence continues from the highest number that has ever been used in that column in that particular table. This is how we did record numbers in preallocated sequential files in the 1950s, by the way. A utility program would then pack or compress the records that were flagged as deleted or unused to move the empty space to the physical end of the physical file.

But we now use a statement with a query expression in it, like this:

```
INSERT INTO Foobar (a, b, c)
SELECT x, y, z
  FROM Floob;
```

Because a query result is a table, and a table is a set that has no ordering, what should the auto-numbers be? The entire, whole, completed set is presented to Foobar all at once, not a row at a time. There are (n!) ways to number (n) rows, so which one do you pick? The answer has been to use whatever the physical order of the result set happened to be. That nonrelational phrase "physical order" again!

But it is actually worse than that. If the same query is executed again, but with new statistics or after an index has been dropped or added, the new execution plan could bring the result set back in a different physical order. Can you explain from a logical model why the same rows in the second query get different auto-numbers? In the relational model, they should be treated the same if all the values of all the attributes are identical.

Using auto-numbering as a primary key is a sign that there is no data model, only an imitation of a sequential file system. Because this magic, all-purpose, one-size-fits-all pseudo identifier exists only as a result of the physical state of a particular piece of hardware, at a particular time, as read by the current release of a particular database product, how do you verify that an entity has such a number in the reality you are modeling? People run into this problem when they have to rebuild their database from scratch after a disaster.

You will see newbies who design tables like this:

```
CREATE Drivers
(driver_id AUTONUMBER NOT NULL PRIMARY KEY,
 ssn CHAR(9) NOT NULL REFERENCES Personnel(ssn),
 vin CHAR(17) NOT NULL REFERENCES Motorpool(vin));
```

Now input data and submit the same row a thousand times or a million times. Your data integrity is trashed. The natural key was this:

```
CREATE Drivers
(ssn CHAR(9) NOT NULL REFERENCES Personnel(ssn),
 vin CHAR(17) NOT NULL REFERENCES Motorpool(vin),
 PRIMARY KEY (ssn, vin));
```

Another problem is that if a natural key exists (which it must, if the data model is correct), then the rows can be updated either through the key or through the auto-number. But because there is no way to reconcile the auto-number and the natural key, you have no data integrity.

To demonstrate, here is a typical newbie schema. I call them "id-iots" because they always name the auto-number column "id" in every table.

```
CREATE TABLE Personnel
(id AUTONUMBER NOT NULL PRIMARY KEY,—false key
 ssn CHAR(9) NOT NULL,—real key
 ..);

INSERT INTO Personnel VALUES ('999999999', ..);
```

Now change a row in Personnel, using the "id" column:

```
UPDATE Personnel
   SET ssn = '666666666'
 WHERE id = 1;
```

or using the natural key:

```
UPDATE Personnel
   SET ssn = '666666666'
 WHERE ssn = '999999999';
```

But when I rebuild the row from scratch:

```
BEGIN ATOMIC
DELETE FROM Personnel WHERE id = 1;
INSERT INTO Personnel VALUES ('666666666', ..);
END;
```

What happened to the tables that referenced Personnel? Imagine a company bowling team table that also had the "id" column and the "ssn" of the players. I need cascaded DRI actions if the "ssn" changes, but I only have the "id," so I have no idea how many "ssn" values the same employee can have. The "id" column is at best redundant, but now we can see that it is also dangerous.

Finally, an appeal to authority, with a quote from Dr. Codd (1979): "Database users may cause the system to generate or delete a surrogate, but they have no control over its value, nor is its value ever displayed to them.

This means that a surrogate ought to act like an index: created by the user, managed by the system, and never seen by a user. That means never used in queries, DRI, or anything else that a user does.

Codd also wrote the following:

> There are three difficulties in employing user-controlled keys as permanent surrogates for entities.
>
> 1. The actual values of user-controlled keys are determined by users and must therefore be subject to change by them (e.g., if two companies merge, the two employee databases might be combined, with the result that some or all of the serial numbers might be changed).
>
> 2. Two relations may have user-controlled keys defined on distinct domains (e.g., one of them uses Social Security, while the other uses employee serial numbers) and yet the entities denoted are the same.
>
> 3. It may be necessary to carry information about an entity either before it has been assigned a user-controlled key value or after it has ceased to have one (e.g., an applicant for a job and a retiree).
>
> These difficulties have the important consequence that an equi-join on common key values may not yield the same result as a join on common entities. A solution—proposed in part [4] and more fully in [14]—is to introduce entity domains, which contain system-assigned surrogates. Database users may cause the system to generate or delete a surrogate, but they have no control over its value, nor is its value ever displayed to them. . . (Codd, 1979).

Exceptions:
If you are using the table as a staging area for data scrubbing or some other purpose than as a database, then feel free to use any kind of proprietary feature you wish to get the data right. We did a lot of this in the early days of RDBMS. Today, however, you should consider using ETL and other software tools that did not exist even a few years ago.

3.14 Do Not Split Attributes

Rationale:
Attribute splitting consists of taking an attribute and modeling it in more than one place in the schema. This violates Domain-key Normal Form

(DKNF) and makes programming insanely difficult. There are several ways to do this, discussed in the following sections.

3.14.1 Split into Tables

The values of an attribute are each given their own table. If you were to do this with gender and have a "MalePersonnel" and a "FemalePersonnel" table, you would quickly see the fallacy. But if I were to split data by years (temporal values) or by location (spatial values) or by department (organizational values), you might not see the same problem.

In order to get any meaningful report, these tables would have to be UNION-ed back into a single "Personnel" table. The bad news is that constraints to prevent overlaps among the tables in the collection can be forgotten or wrong.

Do not confuse attribute splitting with a partitioned table, which is maintained by the system and appears to be a whole to the users.

3.14.2 Split into Columns

The attribute is modeled as a series of columns that make no sense until all of the columns are reassembled (e.g., having a measurement in one column and the unit of measure in a second column). The solution is to have scale and keep all measurements in it.

Look at section 3.3 on BIT data types as one of the worst offenders. You will also see attempts at formatting of long text columns by splitting (e.g., having two 50-character columns instead of one 100-character column so that the physical display code in the front end does not have to calculate a word-wrap function). When you get a 25-character-wide printout, though, you are in trouble.

Another common version of this is to program dynamic domain changes in a table. That is, one column contains the domain, which is metadata, for another column, which is data.

Glenn Carr posted a horrible example of having a column in a table change domain on the fly on September 29, 2004, on the SQL Server programming newsgroup. His goal was to keep football statistics; this is a simplification of his original schema design. I have removed about a dozen other errors in design, so we can concentrate on just the shifting domain problem.

```
CREATE TABLE Player_Stats
(league_id INTEGER NOT NULL,
 player_id INTEGER NOT NULL,—proprietary auto-number on Players
 game_id INTEGER NOT NULL,
 stat_field_id CHAR(20) NOT NULL,—the domain of the number_value
column
 number_value INTEGER NULL,
 ..);
```

The "stat_field_id" held the names of the statistics whose values are given in the "number_value" column of the same row. A better name for this column should have been "yardage_or_completions_or_ interceptions_or_ .." because that is what it has in it.
Here is a rewrite:

```
CREATE TABLE Player_Stats
(league_id INTEGER NOT NULL,
 player_nbr INTEGER NOT NULL,
   FOREIGN KEY (league_id, player_nbr)
   REFERENCES Players (league_id, player_nbr)
   ON UPDATE CASCADE,
 game_id INTEGER NOT NULL
      REFERENCES Games(game_id)
      ON UPDATE CASCADE,
 completions INTEGER DEFAULT 0 NOT NULL CHECK (completions >=
0),
 yards INTEGER DEFAULT 0 NOT NULL CHECK (yards >= 0),
—put other stats here
 ...
 PRIMARY KEY (league_id, player_nbr, game_id));
```

We found by inspection that a player is identified by a (league_id, player_nbr) pair. Player_id was originally another IDENTITY column in the Players table. I see sports games where the jersey of each player has a number; let's use that for identification. If reusing jersey numbers is a problem, then I am sure that leagues have some standard in their industry for this, and I am sure that it is not an auto-incremented number that was set by the hardware in Mr. Carr's machine.

What he was trying to find were composite statistics, such as "Yards per Completion," which is trivial in the rewritten schema. The hardest part of the code is avoiding a division by zero in a calculation. Using the original design, you had to write elaborate self-joins that had awful performance. I leave this as an exercise to the reader.

Exceptions:
This is not really an exception. You can use a column to change the scale, but not the domain, used in another column. For example, I record temperatures in degrees Absolute, Celsius, or Fahrenheit and put the standard abbreviation code in another column. But I have to have a VIEW for each scale used so that I can show Americans everything in Fahrenheit and the rest of the world everything in Celsius. I also want people to be able to update through those views in the units their equipment gives them.

A more complex example would be the use of the ISO currency codes with a decimal amount in a database that keeps international transactions. The domain is constant; the second column is always currency, never shoe size or body temperature. When I do this, I need to have a VIEW that will convert all of the values to the same common currency: Euros, Yen, Dollars, or whatever. But now there is a time element because the exchange rates change constantly. This is not an easy problem.

3.14.3 Split into Rows

The attribute is modeled as a flag and value on each row of the same table. The classic example is temporal, such as this list of events:

```
CREATE TABLE Events
(event_name CHAR(15) NOT NULL,
 event_time TIMESTAMP DEFAULT CURRENT_TIMESRTAMP NOT NULL,
 ..);

INSERT INTO Events
VALUES (('start running', '2005-10-01 12:00:00'),
        ('stop running', '2005-10-01 12:15:13'));
```

Time is measured by duration, not by instants; the correct DDL is:

```
CREATE TABLE Events
(event_name CHAR(15) NOT NULL,
 event_start_time TIMESTAMP DEFAULT CURRENT_TIMESTAMP NOT NULL,
 event_finish_time TIMESTAMP DEFAULT CURRENT_TIMESTAMP NOT NULL,
 CHECK (event_start_time < event_finish_time),
 ..);
```

```
INSERT INTO Events
VALUES ('running', '2005-10-01 12:00:00', '2005-10-01
12:15:13');
```

Exceptions:
None

These are simply bad schema designs that are often the results of confusing the physical representation of the data with the logical model. This tends to be done by older programmers carrying old habits over from file systems.

For example, in the old days of magnetic tape files, the tapes were dated and processing was based on the one-to-one correspondence between time and a physical file. Creating tables with temporal names like "Payroll_Jan," "Payroll_Feb," and so forth just mimic magnetic tapes.

Another source of these errors is mimicking paper forms or input screens directly in the DDL. The most common is an order detail table that includes a line number because the paper form or screen for the order has a line number. Customers buy products that are identified in the inventory database by SKU, UPC, or other codes, not a physical line number on a form on the front of the application. But the programmer splits the quantity attribute into multiple rows.

3.15 Do Not Use Object-Oriented Design for an RDBMS

Rationale:
Many years ago, the INCITS H2 Database Standards Committee (née ANSI X3H2 Database Standards Committee) had a meeting in Rapid City, South Dakota. We had Mount Rushmore and Bjarne Stroustrup as special attractions. Mr. Stroustrup did his slide show about Bell Labs inventing C++ and OO programming for us, and we got to ask questions.

One of the questions was how we should put OO stuff into SQL. His answer was that Bell Labs, with all its talent, had tried four different approaches to this problem and came to the conclusion that you should not do it. OO was great for programming but deadly for data.

3.15.1 A Table Is Not an Object Instance

Tables in a properly designed schema do not appear and disappear like instances of an object. A table represents a set of entities or a relationship. For them to appear (CREATE TABLE) and disappear (DROP TABLE) is like living in a world of magic, where a whole new species of creatures are created by any user, on the fly. Likewise, there are no OIDs in SQL. GUIDs, auto-numbering, and all of those proprietary exposed physical locators will not work in the long run.

I have watched people try to force OO models into SQL, and it falls apart in about a year. Every typo becomes a new attribute, or class queries that would have been so easy in a relational model are now multitable monster outer joins, redundancy grows at an exponential rate, constraints are virtually impossible to write so you can kiss data integrity goodbye, and so on.

In a thread discussing OO versus relational modeling entitled "impedance mismatch" in the comp.databases.theory newsgroup in October 2004, one experienced programmer reported:

> I'm here to tell you what you already know—you are 100 percent correct. I am stuck with working with an OO schema superimposed on an RDBMS. The amount of gymnastics that I need to go through to do what should be the simplest query is unimaginable. It took six man-hours (me and one of the OO developers for three hours) to come up with a query that was the equivalent of:

```
SELECT * FROM Field_Offices;
```

The data needed consisted of basic information, name of the office location, address, manager, and phone. The final query was almost a full page long, required the joining of all the various tables for each data element (as each data element is now an object and each object has its own attributes, so requires its own table), and of course the monster object-linking tables so as to obtain the correct instance of each object.

By the way, which instance is the correct one? Why, the latest one, of course, unless it is marked as not being the one to use, in which case look for the one that is so marked. And the marking indicator is not always the same value, as there are several potential values. These object-linking tables are the biggest in the entire database. Millions of rows in each of these in just one year's time to keep track of less than 80,000 entity instances.

Self-joins are needed in some cases; here are two of these monster tables, and a few smaller ones.

Fortunately, there are extracts that run nightly to transform the data into a relational schema set up for reporting, but not all the data is there, or is wrong, so sometimes I need to go through the above.

3.15.2 Do Not Use EAV Design for an RDBMS

The Entity-Attribute-Value (EAV) design flaw is particularly popular among newbies who come from the agile or extreme school of software development. This school used to be called "Code first, design and think later" when it was first popular.

The idea is that you have one huge table with three columns of metadata: entity name, attribute name, and attribute value. This lets your users invent new entities as they use the database. If the American wants to create something called a "tire" and the British speaker wants to create something called a "tyre," then they are both free to do so.

The values have be recorded in the most general data type in the SQL engine, so you use a lot of VARCHAR(n) columns in the EAV model. Now try to put a constraint on the column.

Exceptions:

None. There are better tools for collecting free-form data.

Scales and Measurements

BEFORE YOU CAN put data into a database, you actually need to think about how it will be represented and manipulated. Most programmers have never heard of measurement theory or thought about the best way to represent their data. Although this topic is not specifically about SQL style, it gives a foundation for decisions that have to be made in the design of any schema.

4.1 Measurement Theory

Measure all that is measurable and attempt to make measurable that which is not yet so.

—Galileo (1564–1642)

Measurement theory is a branch of applied mathematics that is useful in data analysis. Measurements are not the same as the attribute being measured. Measurement is not just assigning numbers to things or their attributes so much as it is assigning to things a structural property that can be expressed in numbers or other computable symbols. This structure is the scale used to take the measurement; the numbers or symbols represent units of measure.

Strange as it might seem, measurement theory came from psychology, not mathematics or computer science. In particular, S. S.

Stevens originated the idea of levels of measurement and classification of scales. Scales are classified into types by the properties they do or do not have. The properties with which we are concerned are the following:

1. *A natural origin point on the scale*. This is sometimes called a zero, but it does not have to be literally a numeric zero. For example, if the measurement is the distance between objects, the natural zero is zero meters—you cannot get any closer than that. If the measurement is the temperature of objects, the natural zero is zero degrees Kelvin—nothing can get any colder than absolute zero. However, consider time: It goes from an eternal past into an eternal future, so you cannot find a natural origin for it.
2. *Meaningful operations can be performed on the units*. It makes sense to add weights together to get a new weight. However, adding names or shoe sizes together is absurd.
3. *A natural ordering of the units*. It makes sense to speak about an event occurring before or after another event, or a thing being heavier, longer, or hotter than another thing, but the alphabetical order imposed on a list of names is arbitrary, not natural—a foreign language, with different names for the same objects, would impose another ordering.
4. *A natural metric function on the units*. A metric function has nothing to do with the metric system of measurements, which is more properly called SI, for Systemé International d'units in French. Metric functions have the following three properties:
   a. The metric between an object and itself is the natural origin of the scale. We can write this in a semimathematical notation as $M(a, a) = 0$.
   b. The order of the objects in the metric function does not matter. Again in the notation, $M(a, b) = M(b, a)$.
   c. There is a natural additive function that obeys the rule that $M(a, b) + M(b, c) = M(a, c)$, which is also known as the *triangular inequality*.

This notation is meant to be more general than just arithmetic. The zero in the first property is the origin of the scale, not just a numeric zero. The third property, defined with a plus and a greater than or equal to sign, is a symbolic way of expressing general ordering relationships. The greater than or equal to sign refers to a natural ordering on the attribute being measured. The plus sign refers to a meaningful operation in regard to that ordering, not just arithmetic addition.

The special case of the third property, where the greater than or equal to is always greater than, is desirable to people because it means that they can use numbers for units and do simple arithmetic with the scales. This is called a *strong metric property*. For example, human perceptions of sound and light intensity follow a cube root law—that is, if you double the intensity of light, the perception of the intensity increases by only 20 percent (Stevens, 1957). The actual formula is "Physical intensity to the 0.3 power equals perceived intensity" in English. Knowing this, designers of stereo equipment use controls that work on a logarithmic scale internally but that show evenly spaced marks on the control panel of the amplifier.

It is possible to have a scale that has any combination of the metric properties. For example, instead of measuring the distance between two places in meters, measure it in units of effort. This is the old Chinese system, which had uphill and downhill units of distance.

Does this system of distances have the property that $M(a, a) = 0$? Yes. It takes no effort to get to where you already are located. Does it have the property that $M(a, b) = M(b, a)$? No. It takes less effort to go downhill than to go uphill. Does it have the property that $M(a, b) + M(b, c) = M(a, c)$? Yes. The amount of effort needed to go directly to a place will always be less than the effort of making another stop along the way.

4.1.1 Range and Granularity

Range and granularity are properties of the way the measurements are made. Because we have to store data in a database within certain limits, these properties are important to a database designer. The types of scales are unrelated to whether you use discrete or continuous variables. Although measurements are always discrete because of finite precision, attributes can be conceptually either discrete or continuous regardless of measurement level. Temperature is usually regarded as a continuous attribute, so temperature measurement to the nearest degree Kelvin is a ratio-level measurement of a continuous attribute. However, quantum mechanics holds that the universe is fundamentally discrete, so temperature may actually be a discrete attribute. In ordinal scales for continuous attributes, ties are impossible (or have probability zero). In ordinal scales for discrete attributes, ties are possible. Nominal scales

usually apply to discrete attributes. Nominal scales for continuous attributes can be modeled but are rarely used.

4.1.2 Range

A scale also has other properties that are of interest to someone building a database. First, scales have a range: What are the highest and lowest values that can appear on the scale? It is possible to have a finite or an infinite limit on either the lower or the upper bound. Overflow and underflow errors are the result of range violations inside the database hardware.

Database designers do not have infinite storage, so we have to pick a subrange to use in the database when we have no upper or lower bound. For example, few computer calendar routines will handle geologic time periods, but then few companies have bills that have been outstanding for that long either, so we do not mind.

4.1.3 Granularity, Accuracy, and Precision

Look at a ruler and a micrometer. They both measure length, using the same scale, but there is a difference. A micrometer is more precise because it has a finer granularity of units. Granularity is a static property of the scale itself—how many notches there are on your ruler. In Europe, all industrial drawings are done in millimeters; the United States has been using 1/32nd of an inch.

Accuracy is how close the measurement comes to the actual value. Precision is a measure of how repeatable a measurement is. Both depend on granularity, but they are not the same things. Human nature says that a number impresses according to the square of the number of decimal places. Hence, some people will use a computer system to express things to as many decimal places as possible, even when it makes no sense. For example, civil engineering in the United States uses decimal feet for road design. Nobody can build a road any more precisely than that, but many civil engineering students turn in work that is expressed in ten-thousandths of a foot. You don't use a micrometer on asphalt! A database often does not give the user a choice of precision for many calculations. In fact, the SQL standards leave the number of decimal places in the results of many arithmetic operations to be defined by the implementation.

The ideas are easier to explain with handgun targets, which are scales to measure the ability of the shooter to put bullets in the center of a target. A bigger target has a wider range compared with a smaller target. A target with more rings has a higher granularity.

Once you start shooting, a group of shots that are closer together is more precise because the shots were more repeatable. A shot group that is closer to the center is more accurate because the shots were closer to the goal. Notice that precision and accuracy are not the same thing! If I have a good gun whose sights are off, I can get a tight cluster that is not near the bull's eye.

4.2 Types of Scales

The lack or presence of precision and accuracy determines the kind of scale you should choose. Scales are either quantitative or qualitative. Quantitative scales are what most people mean when they think of measurements, because these scales can be manipulated and are usually represented as numbers. Qualitative scales attempt to impose an order on an attribute, but they do not allow for computations—just comparisons.

4.2.1 Nominal Scales

The simplest scales are the nominal scales. They simply assign a unique symbol, usually a number or a name, to each member of the set that they attempt to measure. For example, a list of city names is a nominal scale.

Right away we are into philosophical differences, because many people do not consider listing to be measurement. Because no clear property is being measured, that school of thought would tell us this cannot be a scale.

There is no natural origin point for a set, and likewise there is no ordering. We tend to use alphabetic ordering for names, but it makes just as much sense to use frequency of occurrence or increasing size or almost any other attribute that does have a natural ordering.

The only meaningful operation that can be done with such a list is a test for equality—"Is this city New York or not?"—and the answer will be TRUE, FALSE, or UNKNOWN. Nominal scales are common in databases because they are used for unique identifiers, such as names and descriptions.

4.2.2 Categorical Scales

The next simplest scales are the categorical scales. They place an entity into a category that is assigned a unique symbol, usually a number or a

name. For example, the class of animals might be categorized as reptiles, mammals, and so forth. The categories have to be within the same class of things to make sense.

Again, many people do not consider categorizing to be measurement. The categories are probably defined by a large number of properties, and there are two potential problems with them. The first problem is that an entity might fall into one or more categories. For example, a platypus is a furry, warm-blooded, egg-laying animal. Mammals are warm-blooded but give live birth and optionally have fur. The second problem is that an entity might not fall into any of the categories at all. If we find a creature with chlorophyll and fur on Mars, we do not have a category of animals in which to place it.

The two common solutions are either to create a new category of animals (monotremes for the platypus and echidna) or to allow an entity to be a member of more than one category. There is no natural origin point for a collection of subsets, and, likewise, there is no ordering of the subsets. We tend to use alphabetic ordering for names, but it makes just as much sense to use frequency of occurrence or increasing size or almost any other attribute that does have a natural ordering.

The only meaningful operation that can be done with such a scale is a test for membership—"Is this animal a mammal or not?"—which will test either TRUE, FALSE, or UNKNOWN.

4.2.3 Absolute Scales

An absolute scale is a count of the elements in a set. Its natural origin is zero, or the empty set. The count is the ordering (a set of five elements is bigger than a set of three elements, and so on). Addition and subtraction are metric functions. Each element is taken to be identical and interchangeable. For example, when you buy a dozen Grade A eggs, you assume that for your purposes any Grade A egg will do the same job as any other Grade A egg. Again, absolute scales are in databases because they are used for quantities.

4.2.4 Ordinal Scales

Ordinal scales put things in order but have no origin and no operations. For example, geologists use a scale to measure the hardness of minerals called Moh's Scale for Hardness (MSH). It is based on a set of standard minerals, which are ordered by relative hardness (talc = 1, gypsum = 2, calcite = 3, fluorite = 4, apatite = 5, feldspar = 6, quartz = 7, topaz = 8, sapphire = 9, diamond = 10).

To measure an unknown mineral, you try to scratch the polished surface of one of the standard minerals with it; if it scratches the surface, the unknown is harder. Notice that I can get two different unknown minerals with the same measurement that are not equal to each other and that I can get minerals that are softer than my lower bound or harder than my upper bound. There is no origin point, and operations on the measurements make no sense (e.g., if I add 10 talc units, I do not get a diamond).

Perhaps the most common use we see of ordinal scales today is to measure preferences or opinions. You are given a product or a situation and asked to decide how much you like or dislike it, how much you agree or disagree with a statement, and so forth. The scale is usually given a set of labels such as "strongly agree" through "strongly disagree," or the labels are ordered from 1 to 5.

Consider pairwise choices between ice cream flavors. Saying that vanilla is preferred over wet leather in our taste test might well be expressing a universal truth, but there is no objective unit of likeability to apply. The lack of a unit means that such things as opinion polls that try to average such scales are meaningless; the best you can do is a bar graph of the number of respondents in each category.

Another problem is that an ordinal scale may not be transitive. *Transitivity* is the property of a relationship in which if $R(a, b)$ and $R(b, c)$, then $R(a, c)$. We like this property and expect it in the real world, where we have relationships like "heavier than," "older than," and so forth. This is the result of a strong metric property.

But an ice cream taster, who has just found out that the shop is out of vanilla, might prefer squid over wet leather, wet leather over wood, and wood over squid, so there is no metric function or linear ordering at all. Again, we are into philosophical differences, because many people do not consider a nontransitive relationship to be a scale.

4.2.5 Rank Scales

Rank scales have an origin and an ordering but no natural operations. The most common example of this would be military ranks. Nobody is lower than a private, and that rank is a starting point in your military career, but it makes no sense to somehow combine three privates to get a sergeant.

Rank scales have to be transitive: A sergeant gives orders to a private, and because a major gives orders to a sergeant, he or she can also give orders to a private. You will see ordinal and rank scales grouped together in some of the literature if the author does not allow nontransitive

ordinal scales. You will also see the same fallacies committed when people try to do statistical summaries of such scales.

4.2.6 Interval Scales

Interval scales have a metric function, ordering, and meaningful operations among the units but no natural origin. Calendars are the best example; some arbitrary historical event is the starting point for the scale and all measurements are related to it using identical units or intervals. Time, then, extends from a past eternity to a future eternity.

The metric function is the number of days between two dates. Look at the three properties: (1) $M(a, a) = 0$: there are zero days between today and today; (2) $M(a, b) = M(b, a)$: there are just as many days from today to next Monday as there are from next Monday to today; and (3) $M(a, b) + M(b, c) = M(a, c)$: the number of days from today to next Monday plus the number of days from next Monday to Christmas is the same as the number of days from today until Christmas. Ordering is natural and strong: 1900-July-1 occurs before 1993-July-1. Aggregations of the basic unit (days) into other units (weeks, months, and years) are also arbitrary.

Please do not think that the only metric function is simple math; there are log-interval scales, too. The measurements are assigned numbers such that ratios between the numbers reflect ratios of the attribute. You then use formulas of the form ($c \times m$^d), where c and d are constants, to do transforms and operations. For example, density = (mass/volume), fuel efficiency expressed in miles per gallon (mpg), decibel scale for sound, and the Richter scale for earthquakes are exponential, so their functions involve logarithms and exponents.

4.2.7 Ratio Scales

Ratio scales are what people think of when they think about a measurement. Ratio scales have an origin (usually zero units), an ordering, and a set of operations that can be expressed in arithmetic. They are called ratio scales because all measurements are expressed as multiples or fractions of a certain unit or interval.

Length, mass, and volume are examples of this type of scale. The unit is what is arbitrary: The weight of a bag of sand is still weight whether it is measured in kilograms or in pounds. Another nice property is that the units are identical: A kilogram is still a kilogram whether it is measuring feathers or bricks.

4.3 Using Scales

Absolute and ratio scales are also called extensive scales because they deal with quantities, as opposed to the remaining scales, which are intensive because they measure qualities. Quantities can be added and manipulated together, whereas qualities cannot. Table 4.1 describes the different types of scales and their attributes.

Table 4.1 *Scale properties*

Type of Scale	Natural Ordering	Natural Origin	Functions	Example
Nominal	No	No	No	City names ("Atlanta")
Categorical	No	No	No	Species (dog, cat)
Absolute	Yes	Yes	Yes	Eggs (dozen)
Ordinal	Yes	No	No	Preferences (agree 1 to 5 scale)
Rank	Yes	Yes	No	Contests (win, place, show)
Interval	Yes	No	Yes	Time (hours, minutes)
Ratio	Yes	Yes	Yes	Length (meters), Mass (grams)

The origin for the absolute scale is numeric zero, and the natural functions are simple arithmetic. However, things are not always this simple. Temperature has an origin point at absolute zero, and its natural functions average heat over mass. This is why you cannot defrost a refrigerator, which is at 0 degrees Celsius, by putting a chicken whose body temperature is 35 degrees Celsius inside of it. The chicken does not have enough mass relative to heat. However, a bar of white-hot steel will do a nice job.

4.4 Scale Conversion

Scales can be put in a partial order based on the permissible transformations:

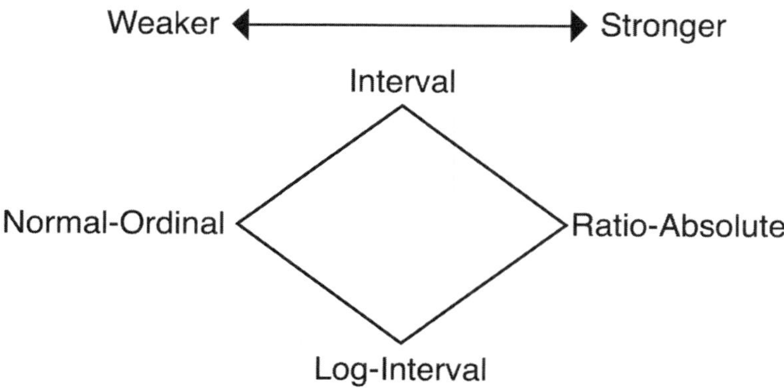

An attribute might not fit exactly into any of these scales. For example, you mix nominal and ordinal information in a single scale, such as in questionnaires that have several nonresponse categories. It is common to have scales that mix ordinal and an interval scale by assuming the attribute is really a smooth monotone function. Subjective rating scales ("strongly agree," "agree," . . . "strongly disagree") have no equally spaced intervals between the ratings, but there are statistical techniques to ensure that the difference between two intervals is within certain limits. A binary variable is at least an interval scale, and it might be a ratio or absolute scale, if it means that the attribute exists or does not exist.

The important principle of measurement theory is that you can convert from one scale to another only if they are of the same type and measure the same attribute. Absolute scales do not convert, which is why they are called absolute scales. Five apples are five apples, no matter how many times you count them or how you arrange them on the table. Nominal scales are converted to other nominal scales by a mapping between the scales.

That means you look things up in a table. For example, I can convert my English city names to Polish city names with a dictionary. The problem comes when there is not a one-to-one mapping between the two nominal scales. For example, English uses the word "cousin" to identify the offspring of your parents' siblings, and tradition treats them all pretty much alike.

Chinese language and culture have separate words for the same relations based on the genders of your parents' siblings and the age relationships among them (e.g., the oldest son of your father's oldest brother is a particular type of cousin and you have different social obligations to him). Something is lost in translation.

Ordinal scales are converted to ordinal scales by a monotone function. That means you preserve the ordering when you convert. Looking at the MSH for geologists, I can pick another set of minerals, plastics, or metals to scratch, but rock samples that were definitely softer than others are still softer. Again, there are problems when there is not a one-to-one mapping between the two scales. My new scale may be able to tell the difference between rocks, whereas the MSH could not.

Rank scales are converted to rank scales by a monotone function that preserves the ordering, like ordinal scales. Again, there are problems when there is not a one-to-one mapping between the two scales. For example, different military branches have slightly different ranks that don't quite correspond to each other.

In both the nominal and the ordinal scales, the problem was that things that looked equal on one scale were different on another. This has to do with range and granularity, which was discussed in section 4.1.1 of this chapter.

Interval scales are converted to interval scales by a linear function; that is, a function of the form $y = a \times x + b$. This preserves the ordering but shifts the origin point when you convert. For example, I can convert temperature from degrees Celsius to degrees Fahrenheit using the formula F = (9.0 ÷ 5.0 × C) + 32.

Ratio scales are converted to ratio scales by a constant multiplier, because both scales have the same ordering and origin point. For example, I can convert from pounds to kilograms using the formula p = 0.4536 × k. This is why people like to use ratio scales.

4.5 Derived Units

Many of the scales that we use are not primary units but rather derived units. These measures are constructed from primary units, such as miles per hour (time and distance) or square miles (distance and distance). You can use only ratio and interval scales to construct derived units.

If you use an absolute scale with a ratio or interval scale, you are dealing with statistics, not measurements. For example, using weight (ratio scale) and the number of people in New York (absolute scale), we can compute the average weight of a New Yorker, which is a statistic, not a unit of measurement.

The SI measurements use a basic set of seven units (i.e., meter for length, kilogram for mass, second for time, ampere for electrical current, degree Kelvin for temperature, mole for molecules, and candela for light) and construct derived units. ISO standard 2955 ("Information

processing—Representation of SI and other units for use in systems with limited character sets") has a notation for expressing SI units in ASCII character strings. (See ISO-2955, "Representation of SI and other units for use in systems with limited character sets") The notation uses parentheses, spaces, multiplication (shown by a period), division (shown by a solidus, or slash), and exponents (shown by numerals immediately after the unit abbreviation). There are also names for most of the standard derived units. For example, "100 kg.m ÷ s^2" converts to 10 Newtons (the unit of force), written as "10 N" instead.

4.6 Punctuation and Standard Units

A database stores measurements as numeric data represented in a binary format, but when the data is input or output, a human being wants readable characters and punctuation. Punctuation identifies the units being used and can be used for prefix, postfix, or infix symbols. It can also be implicit or explicit.

If I write $25.15, you know that the unit of measure is the dollar because of the explicit prefix dollar sign. If I write 160 lbs., you know that the unit of measure is pounds because of the explicit postfix abbreviation for the unit. If I write 1989 MAR 12, you know that this is a date because of the implicit infix separation among month, day, and year, achieved by changing from numerals to letters, and the optional spaces. The ISO and SQL defaults represent the same date, using explicit infix punctuation, with 1989-03-12 instead. Likewise, a column header on a report that gives the units used is explicit punctuation.

Databases do not generally store punctuation. The sole exception might be the proprietary MONEY or CURRENCY data type found in many SQL implementations as a vendor extension. Punctuation wastes storage space, and the units can be represented in some internal format that can be used in calculations. Punctuation is only for display.

It is possible to put the units in a column next to a numeric column that holds their quantities, but this is awkward and wastes storage space. If everything is expressed in the same unit, the units column is redundant. If things are expressed in different units, you have to convert them to a common unit to do any calculations. Why not store them in a common unit in the first place? The DBA has to be sure that all data in a column of a table is expressed in the same units before it is stored. There are some horror stories about multinational companies sending the same input programs used in the United States to their European offices, where SI and English measurements were mixed into the same database without conversion.

Ideally, the DBA should be sure that data is kept in the same units in all the tables in the database. If different units are needed, they can be provided in a VIEW that hides the conversions (thus the office in the United States sees English measurements and the European offices see SI units and date formats; neither is aware of the conversions being done for it).

4.7 General Guidelines for Using Scales in a Database

The following are general guidelines for using measurements and scales in a database and not firm, hard rules. You will find exceptions to all of them.

1. *In general, the more unrestricted the permissible transformations on a scale are, the more restricted the statistics.* Almost all statistics are applicable to measurements made on ratio scales, but only a limited group of statistics may be applied to measurements made on nominal scales.

2. *Use CHECK() clauses on table declarations to make sure that only the allowed values appear in the database.* If you have the CREATE DOMAIN feature of SQL-92, use it to build your scales. Nominal scales would have a list of possible values; other scales would have range checking. Likewise, use the DEFAULT clauses to be sure that each scale starts with its origin value, a NULL, or a default value that makes sense.

3. *Declare at least one more decimal place than you think you will need for your smallest units.* In most SQL implementations, rounding and truncation will improve with more decimal places.

   The downside of SQL is that precision and the rules for truncation and rounding are implementation dependent, so a query with calculations might not give the same results on another product. However, SQL is more merciful than older file systems, because the DBA can ALTER a numeric column so it will have more precision and a greater range without destroying existing data or queries. Host programs may have to be changed to display the extra characters in the results, however.

You also need to consider laws and accounting rules that deal with currencies. The European Union has rules for computing with euros, and the United States has similar rules for dollars in the Generally Accepted Accounting Practices (GAAP).

4. *Try to store primary units rather than derived units*. This is not always possible, because you might not be able to measure anything but the derived unit. Look at your new tire gauge; it is set for Pascal (Newtons per square meter) and will not tell you how many square meters you have on the surface of the tire or the force exerted by the air, and you simply cannot figure these things out from the Pascals given. A set of primary units can be arranged in many different ways to construct any possible derived unit desired. Never store both the derived and the primary units in the same table. Not only is this redundant, but it opens the door to possible errors when a primary-unit column is changed and the derived units based on it are not updated. Also, most computers can recalculate the derived units much faster than they can read a value from a disk drive.

5. *Use the same punctuation whenever a unit is displayed*. For example, do not mix ISO and ANSI date formats, or express weight in pounds and kilograms in the same report. Ideally, everything should be displayed in the same way in the entire application system.

Data Encoding Schemes

YOU DO NOT put data directly into a database. You convert it into an encoding scheme first, then put the encoding into the rows of the tables. Words have to be written in an alphabet and belong to a language; measurements are expressed as numbers. We are so used to seeing words and numbers that we no longer think of them as encoding schemes. We also often fail to distinguish among the possible ways to identify (and therefore to encode) an entity or property. Do we encode the person receiving medical services or the policy that is paying for them? That might depend on whether the database is for the doctor or for the insurance company. Do we encode the first title of a song or the alternate title, or both? Or should we include the music itself in a multimedia database? And should it be as an image of the sheet music or as an audio recording? Nobody teaches people how to design these encoding schemes, so they are all too often done on the fly. Where standardized encoding schemes exist, they are too often ignored in favor of some ad hoc scheme. Beginning programmers have the attitude that encoding schemes do not really matter because the computer will take care of it, so they don't have to spend time on the design of their encoding schemes. This attitude has probably gotten worse with SQL than it was before. The new database designer thinks that an ALTER statement can fix any bad things he or she did at the start of the project.

Yes, the computer can take care of a lot of problems, but the data entry and validation programs become complex and difficult to maintain. Database queries that have to follow the same convoluted encodings will cost both computer time and money, and a human being still has to use the code at some point. Bad schemes result in errors in data entry and misreading of outputs and can lead to incorrect data models.

5.1 Bad Encoding Schemes

To use an actual example, the automobile tag system for a certain southern state started as a punchcard system written in COBOL. Many readers are likely too young to remember punchcard (keypunch) machines. A punchcard is a piece of stiff paper on which a character is represented as one or more rectangular holes made into one of 80 vertical columns on the card. Contiguous groups of columns make up fixed-length fields of data. The keypunch machine has a typewriter-like keyboard; it automatically feeds cards into the punch as fast as a human being can type. The position, length, and alphabetic or numeric shift for each field on the card can be set by a control card in the keypunch machine to save the operator keystrokes. This is a fixed format and a fast input method, and making changes to a program once it is in place is difficult.

The auto tag system had a single card column for a single-position numeric code to indicate the type of tag: private car, chauffeured car, taxi, truck, public bus, and so forth. As time went on, more tag types were added for veterans of assorted wars, for university alumni, and for whatever other lobbyist group happened to have the political power to pass a bill allowing it a special auto tag.

Soon there were more than 10 types, so a single-digit system could not represent them. There was room on the punchcard to change the length of the field to two digits, but COBOL uses fixed-length fields, so changing the card layout would require changes in the programs and in the keypunch procedures.

The first new tag code was handled by letting the data-entry clerk press a punctuation-mark key instead of changing from numeric lock to manual shift mode. Once that decision was made, it was followed for each new code thereafter, until the scheme looked like everything on the upper row of keys on a typewriter.

Unfortunately, different makes and models of keypunch machines have different punctuation marks in the same keyboard position, so each deck of cards had to have a special program to convert its punches to the original model IBM 026 keypunch codes before the master file was updated. This practice continued even after all of the original machines had been retired to used-equipment heaven.

The edit programs could not check for a simple numeric range to validate input but had to use a small lookup routine with more than 20 values in it. That does not sound like much until you realize that the system had to handle more than 3 million records in the first quarter of the year. The error rate was high, and each batch needed to know which machine had punched the cards before it could use a lookup table.

If the encoding scheme had been designed with two digits (00 to 99) at the beginning, all of the problems would have been avoided. If I were to put this system into a database today, using video terminals for data entry, the tag type could be INTEGER and it could hold as many tag types as I would ever need. This is part of the legacy database problem.

The second example was reported in *Information Systems Week* in 1987. The first sentence told the whole story: "The chaos and rampant error rates in New York City's new Welfare Management System appear to be due to a tremendous increase in the number of codes it requires in data entry and the subsequent difficulty for users in learning to use it." The rest of the article explained how the new system attempted to merge several old existing systems. In the merger, the error rates increased from 2 percent to more than 20 percent because the encoding schemes used could not be matched up and consolidated.

How do you know a bad encoding scheme when you see one? One bad feature is the failure to allow for growth. Talk to anyone who had to reconfigure a fixed-length record system to allow for the change from the old ZIP codes to the current ZIP+4 codes in their address data. SQL does not have this as a physical problem, but it can show up as a logical problem.

Another bad property is ambiguous encodings in the scheme. Perhaps the funniest example of this problem was the Italian telephone system's attempt at a "time of day" service. It used a special three-digit number, like the 411 information number in the United States, but the three digits they picked were also those of a telephone exchange in Milan, so nobody could call into that exchange without getting the time signal before they completed their call.

This happens more often than you would think, but the form that it usually takes is that of a miscellaneous code that is too general. Very different cases are then encoded as identical, and the user is given incorrect or misleading information when a query is performed.

A bad encoding scheme lacks codes for missing, unknown, not applicable, or miscellaneous values. The classic story is the man who bought a prestige auto tag reading "NONE" and got thousands of traffic tickets as a result. The police had no special provision for a missing tag on the tickets, so when a car had no tag, they wrote "none" in the field for the tag number. The database simply matched his name and address to every unpaid missing-tag ticket on file at the time.

Before you say that the NULL in SQL is a quick solution to this problem, think about how NULL is ignored in many SQL functions. The SQL query "SELECT tag_nbr, SUM(fine) FROM tickets GROUP BY tag_nbr;" will give the total fines on each car, but it also puts all of the missing tags into one group (i.e., one car), although we want to see each one as a separate case, because it is unlikely that there is only one untagged car in all of California.

There are also differences among "missing," "unknown," "not applicable," "miscellaneous," and erroneous values that are subtle but important. For example, the International Classification of Disease uses 999.999 for miscellaneous illness. It means that we have diagnosed the patient, know that he or she has an illness, and cannot classify it—a scary condition for the patient—but this is not quite the same thing as a missing disease code (just admitted, might not even be sick), an inapplicable disease code (pregnancy complications in a male), an unknown disease code (sick and awaiting lab results), or an error in the diagnosis (the patient's temperature is recorded as 100 degrees Celsius, not Fahrenheit).

5.2 Encoding Scheme Types

The following is my classification system for encoding schemes and suggestions for using each of them. You will find some of these same ideas in library science and other fields, but I have never seen anyone else attempt a classification system for data processing.

5.2.1 Enumeration Encoding

An enumeration encoding arranges the attribute values in some order and assigns a number or a letter to each value. Numbers are usually a better choice than letters, because they can be increased without limit as more values are added. Enumeration schemes are a good choice for a short list of values but a bad choice for a long list. It is too difficult to remember a long list of codes, and soon any natural ordering principle is violated as new values are tacked onto the end.

A good heuristic is to order the values in some natural manner, if one exists in the data, so that table lookup will be easier. Chronological order (1 occurs before 2) or procedural order (1 must be done before 2) is often a good choice. Another good heuristic is to order the values from most common to least common. That way you will have shorter codes for the most common cases. Other orderings could be based on physical characteristics such as largest to smallest, rainbow-color order, and so on.

After arguing for a natural order in the list, I must admit that the most common scheme is alphabetical order, because it is simple to implement on a computer and makes it easy for a person to look up values in a table. ANSI standard X3.31, "Structure for the Identification of Counties of the United States for Information Interchange," encodes county names within a state by first alphabetizing the names, and then numbering them from one to whatever is needed.

5.2.2 Measurement Encoding

A measurement encoding is given in some unit of measure, such as pounds, meters, volts, or liters. This can be done in one of two ways. The column contains an implied unit of measure and the numbers represent the quantity in that unit, but sometimes the column explicitly contains the unit. The most common example of the second case would be money fields, where a dollar sign is used in the column; you know that the unit is dollars, not pounds or yen, by the sign.

Scales and measurement theory are a whole separate topic and are discussed in detail in Chapter 4.

5.2.3 Abbreviation Encoding

Abbreviation codes shorten the attribute values to fit into less storage space, but the reader easily understands them. The codes can be either of fixed length or of variable length, but computer people tend to prefer fixed length. The most common example is the two-letter postal state abbreviations (e.g., CA for California, AL for Alabama), which replaced the old variable-length abbreviations (Calif. for California, Ala. for Alabama).

A good abbreviation scheme is handy, but as the set of values becomes larger, the possibility for misunderstanding increases. The three-letter codes for airport baggage are pretty obvious for major cities: LAX for Los Angeles, SFO for San Francisco, BOS for Boston, ATL for

Atlanta, but nobody can figure out the abbreviations for the smaller airports.

As another example, consider the ISO 3166 Country Codes, which come in two-letter, three-letter, and nonabbreviation numeric forms. The RIPE Network Coordination Centre maintains these codes.

5.2.4 Algorithmic Encoding

Algorithmic encoding takes the value to be encoded and puts it through an algorithm to obtain the encodings. The algorithm should be reversible, so that the original value can be recovered. Although it is not required, the encoding is usually shorter (or at least of known maximum size) and more uniform in some useful way compared with the original value. Encryption is the most common example of an algorithmic encoding scheme, but it is so important that it needs to be considered as a topic by itself.

Computer people are used to using Julianized dates, which convert a date into an integer. As an aside, please note that astronomers used the *Julian Date*, which is a large number that represents the number of days since a particular heavenly event. The Julianized date is a number between 1 and 365 or 366, which represents the ordinal position of the day within the year. Algorithms take up computer time in both data input and output, but the encoding is useful because it allows searching or calculations to be done that would be difficult using the original data. Julianized dates can be used for computations; Soundex names give a phonetic matching that would not be possible with the original text.

Another example is hashing functions, which convert numeric values into other numeric values for placing them in storage and retrieving them. Rounding numeric values before they go into the database is also a case of algorithmic encoding.

The difference between an abbreviation and an algorithm is not that clear. An abbreviation can be considered a special case of an algorithm, which tells you how to remove or replace letters. The tests to tell them apart are as follows:

1. When a human being can read it without effort, it is an abbreviation.
2. An algorithmic encoding is not easily human readable.
3. An algorithmic encoding might return the same code for more than one value, but an abbreviation is always one-to-one.

5.2.5 Hierarchical Encoding Schemes

A hierarchy partitions the set of values into disjoint categories, then partitions those categories into subcategories, and so forth until some final level is reached. Such schemes are shown either as nested sets or as tree charts. Each category has some meaning in itself, and the subcategories refine meaning further.

The most common example is the ZIP code, which partitions the United States geographically. Each digit, as you read from left to right, further isolates the location of the address: first by postal region, then by state, then by city, and finally by the post office that has to make the delivery. For example, given the ZIP code 30310, we know that the 30000 to 39999 range means the southeastern United States. Within the southeastern codes, we know that the 30000 to 30399 range is Georgia and that 30300 to 30399 is metropolitan Atlanta. Finally, the whole code, 30310, identifies substation A in the West End section of the city. The ZIP code can be parsed by reading it from left to right, reading first one digit, then two, and then the last two digits.

Another example is the Dewey Decimal Classification (DDC) system, which is used in public libraries in the United States. The 500-number series covers "Natural Sciences"; within that, the 510s cover "Mathematics"; and, finally, 512 deals with "Algebra" in particular. The scheme could be carried further, with decimal fractions for kinds of algebra.

Hierarchical encoding schemes are great for large data domains that have a natural hierarchy. They organize the data for searching and reporting along that natural hierarchy and make it easy, but there can be problems in designing these schemes. First, the tree structure does not have to be neatly balanced, so some categories may need more codes than others and hence create more breakdowns. Eastern and ancient religions are shortchanged in the Dewey Decimal Classification system, reflecting a prejudice toward Christian and Jewish writings. Asian religions were pushed into a very small set of codes. Today, the Library of Congress has more books on Buddhist thought than on any other religion on earth.

Second, you might not have made the right choices as to where to place certain values in the tree. For example, in the Dewey Decimal system, books on logic are encoded as 164, in the philosophy section, and not under the 510s, mathematics. In the 19th century, there was no mathematical logic. Today, nobody would think of looking for logic under philosophy. Dewey was simply following the conventions of his

day, and, like today's programmers, he found that the system specifications changed while he was working.

5.2.6 Vector Encoding

A vector is made up of a fixed number of components. These components can be ordered or unordered, but are always present. They can be of fixed or variable length. The components can be dependent or independent of each other, but the code applies to a single entity and makes sense only as a whole unit. Punctuation, symbol-set changes, or position within the code can determine the components of the vector.

The most common example is a date, whose components are month, day, and year. The parts have some meaning by themselves, but the real meaning is in the vector—the date—as a whole because it is a complete entity. The different date formats used in computer systems give examples of all the options. The three components can be written in year-month-day order, month-day-year order, or just about any other way you wish.

The limits on the values for the day depend on the year (is it a leap year or not?) and the month (28, 29, 30, or 31 days?). The components can be separated by punctuation (12/1/2005, using slashes and American date format), symbol-set changes (2005 DEC 01, using digits-letters-digits), or position (20051201, using positions 1 to 4, 5 to 6, and 7 to 8 for year, month, and day, respectively).

Another example is the ISO code for tire sizes, which is made up of a wheel diameter (scaled in inches), a tire type (abbreviation code), and a width (scaled in centimeters). Thus, 15R155 means a 15-inch radial tire that is 155 millimeters wide, whereas 15SR155 is a steel-belted radial tire with the same dimensions. Despite the mixed American and ISO units, this is a general physical description of a tire in a single code.

Vector schemes are informative and allow you to pick the best scheme for each component, but they have to be disassembled to get to the components (many database products provide special functions to do this for dates, street addresses, and people's names). Sorting by components is difficult unless you want them in the order given in the encoding; try to sort the tire sizes by construction, width, and diameter instead of by diameter, construction, and width.

Another disadvantage is that a bad choice in one component can destroy the usefulness of the whole scheme. Another problem is extending the code. For example, if the standard tire number had to be expanded to include thickness in millimeters, where would that measurement go? Another number would have to be separated by a punctuation mark. It could not be inserted into a position inside the code without giving ambiguous codes. The code cannot be easily converted to a fixed-position vector encoding without changing many of the database routines.

5.2.7 Concatenation Encoding

A concatenation code is made up of a variable number of components that are concatenated together. As in a vector encoding, the components can be ordered or unordered, dependent on or independent of each other, and determined by punctuation, symbol-set changes, or position.

A concatenation code is often a hierarchy that is refined by additions to the right. These are also known as *facet codes* in Europe. Or the code can be a list of features, any of which can be present or missing. The order of the components may or may not be important.

Concatenation codes were popular in machine shops at the turn of the 20th century: A paper tag was attached to a piece of work, and workers at different stations would sign off on their parts of the manufacturing process. Concatenation codes are still used in parts of the airplane industry, where longer codes represent subassemblies of the assembly in the head (also called the root or parent) of the code.

Another type of concatenation code is a quorum code, which is not ordered. These codes say that n out of k marks must be present for the code to have meaning. For example, three out of five inspectors must approve a part before it passes.

The most common use of concatenation codes is in keyword lists in the header records of documents in textbases. The author or librarian assigns each article in the system a list of keywords that describes the material covered by the article. The keywords are picked from a limited, specialized vocabulary that belongs to a particular discipline.

Concatenation codes fell out of general use because their variable length made them more difficult to store in older computer systems, which used fixed-length records (think of a punchcard). The codes had to be ordered and stored as left-justified strings to sort correctly.

These codes could also be ambiguous if they were poorly designed. For example, is the head of 1234 the 1 or the 12 substring? When concatenation codes are used in databases, they usually become a set of yes/no checkboxes, represented as adjacent columns in the file. This makes them Boolean vector codes, instead of true concatenation codes.

5.3 General Guidelines for Designing Encoding Schemes

These are general guidelines for designing encoding schemes in a database, not firm, hard rules. You will find exceptions to all of them.

5.3.1 Existing Encoding Standards

The use of existing standard encoding schemes is always recommended. If everyone uses the same codes, data will be easy to transfer and collect uniformly. Also, someone who sat down and did nothing else but work on this scheme probably did a better job than you could while trying to get a database up and running.

As a rule of thumb, if you don't know the industry in which you are working, ask a subject-area expert. Although that sounds obvious, I have worked on a media library database project where the programmers actively avoided talking to the professional librarians who were on the other side of the project. As a result, recordings were keyed on GUIDs and there were no Schwann catalog numbers in the system. If you cannot find an expert, then Google for standards. First, check to see if ISO has a standard, then check the U.S. government, and then check industry groups and organizations.

5.3.2 Allow for Expansion

Allow for expansion of the codes. The ALTER statement can create more storage when a single-character code becomes a two-character code, but it will not change the spacing on the printed reports and screens. Start with at least one more decimal place or character position than you think you will need. Visual psychology makes "01" look like an encoding, whereas "1" looks like a quantity.

5.3.3 Use Explicit Missing Values to Avoid NULLs

Rationale:

Avoid using NULLs as much as possible by putting special values in the encoding scheme instead. SQL handles NULLs differently than values, and NULLs don't tell you what kind of missing value you are dealing with.

All-zeros are often used for missing values and all-nines for miscellaneous values. For example, the ISO gender codes are 0 = Unknown, 1 = Male, 2 = Female, and 9 = Not Applicable. "Not applicable" means a lawful person, such as a corporation, which has no gender.

Versions of FORTRAN before the 1977 standard read blank (unpunched) columns in punchcards as zeros, so if you did not know a value, you skipped those columns and punched them later, when you did know. Likewise, using encoding schemes with leading zeros was a security trick to prevent blanks in a punchcard from being altered. The FORTRAN 77 standard fixed its "blank versus zero" problem, but it lives on in SQL in poorly designed systems that cannot tell a NULL from a blank string, an empty string, or a zero.

The use of all-nines or all-Z's for miscellaneous values will make those values sort to the end of the screen or report. NULLs sort either always to the front or always to the rear, but which way they sort is implementation defined.

Exceptions:
NULLs cannot be avoided. For example, consider the column "termination_date" in the case of a newly hired employee. The use of a NULL makes computations easier and correct. The code simply leaves the NULL date or uses COALESCE (some_date, CURRENT_TIMESTAMP) as is appropriate.

5.3.4 Translate Codes for the End User

As much as possible, avoid displaying pure codes to users, but try to provide a translation for them. Translation in the front is not required for all codes, if they are common and well known to users. For example, most people do not need to see the two-letter state abbreviation written out in words. At the other extreme, however, nobody could read the billing codes used by several long-distance telephone companies.

A part of translation is formatting the display so that it can be read by a human being. Punctuation marks, such as dashes, commas, currency signs, and so forth, are important. However, in a tiered architecture, display is done in the front end, not the database. Trying to put leading zeros or adding commas to numeric values is a common newbie error. Suddenly, everything is a string and you lose all temporal and numeric computation ability.

These translation tables are one kind of auxiliary table; we will discuss other types later. They do not model an entity or relationship in the schema but are used like a function call in a procedural language. The general form for these tables is:

```
CREATE TABLE SomeCodes
(encode <datatype> NOT NULL PRIMARY KEY,
 definition <datatype> NOT NULL);
```

Sometimes you might see the definition as part of the primary key or a CHECK() constraint on the "encode" column, but because these are read-only tables, which are maintained outside of the application, we generally do not worry about having to check their data integrity in the application.

5.3.4.1 One True Lookup Table

Sometimes a practice is both so common and so stupid that it gets a name, and, much like a disease, if it is really bad, it gets an abbreviation. I first ran into the One True Lookup Table (OTLT) design flaw in a thread on a CompuServe forum in 1998, but I have seen it rediscovered in newsgroups every year since.

Instead of keeping the encodings and their definition in one table each, we put all of the encodings in one huge table. The schema for this table was like this:

```
CREATE TABLE OneTrueLookupTable
(code_type INTEGER NOT NULL,
 encoding VARCHAR(n) NOT NULL,
 definition VARCHAR(m) NOT NULL,
 PRIMARY KEY (code_type, encoding));
```

In practice, *m* and *n* are usually something like 255 or 50—default values particular to their SQL product.

The rationale for having all encodings in one table is that it would let the programmer write a single front-end program to maintain all of the encodings. This method really stinks, and I strongly discourage it. Without looking at the following paragraphs, sit down and make a list of all the disadvantages of this method and see if you found anything that I missed. Then read the following list:

1. *Normalization*. The real reason that this approach does not work is that it is an attempt to violate first normal form. I can see that these tables have a primary key and that all of the columns in a SQL database have to be scalar and of one data type, but I will still argue that it is not a first normal form table. The fact that two domains use the same data type does not make them the same attribute. The extra "code_type" column changes the domain of the other columns and thus violates first normal form because the column in not atomic. A table should

model one set of entities or one relationship, not hundreds of them. As Aristotle said, "To be is to be something in particular; to be nothing in particular is to be nothing."

2. *Total storage size*. The total storage required for the OTLT is greater than the storage required for the one encoding, one table approach because of the redundant encoding type column. Imagine having the entire International Classification of Diseases (ICD) and the Dewey Decimal system in one table. Only the needed small single encoding tables have to be put into main storage with single auxiliary tables, while the entire OTLT has to be pulled in and paged in and out of main storage to jump from one encoding to another.

3. *Data types*. All encodings are forced into one data type, which has to be a string of the largest length that any encoding—present and future—used in the system, but VARCHAR(n) is not always the best way to represent data. The first thing that happens is that someone inserts a huge string that looks right on the screen but has trailing blanks or an odd character to the far right side of the column. The table quickly collects garbage.

   CHAR(n) data often has advantages for access and storage in many SQL products. Numeric encodings can take advantage of arithmetic operators for ranges, check digits, and so forth with CHECK() clauses. Dates can be used as codes that are translated into holidays and other events. Data types are not a one-size-fits-all affair. If one encoding allows NULLs, then all of them must in the OTLT.

4. *Validation*. The only way to write a CHECK() clause on the OTLT is with a huge CASE expression of the form:

```
CREATE TABLE OneTrueLookupTable
(code_type CHAR(n) NOT NULL
          CHECK (code_type IN (<type 1>, ..., <type n>)),
 encoding VARCHAR(n) NOT NULL
          CHECK (CASE WHEN code_type = <type 1>
                           AND <validation 1>
                      THEN 1
                        ...
          —assume that your SQL product can support a huge
CASE expression
                      WHEN code_type = <type n>
```

```
                    AND <validation n>
                THEN 1
                ELSE 0 END = 1),
definition VARCHAR(m) NOT NULL,
PRIMARY KEY (code_type, encoding));
```

This means that validation is going to take a long time, because every change will have to be considered by all the WHEN clauses in this oversized CASE expression until the SQL engine finds one that tests TRUE. You also need to add a CHECK() clause to the "code_type" column to be sure that the user does not create an invalid encoding name.

5. *Flexibility*. The OTLT is created with one column for the encoding, so it cannot be used for (n) valued encodings where ($n > 1$). For example, if I want to translate (longitude, latitude) pairs into a location name, I would have to carry an extra column.

6. *Maintenance*. Different encodings can use the same value, so you constantly have to watch which encoding you are working with. For example, both the ICD and Dewey Decimal system have three digits, a decimal point, and three digits.

7. *Security*. To avoid exposing rows in one encoding scheme to unauthorized users, the OTLT has to have VIEWs defined on it that restrict users to the "code_type"s they are allowed to update. At this point, some of the rationale for the single table is gone, because the front end must now handle VIEWs in almost the same way it would handle multiple tables. These VIEWs also have to have the WITH CHECK OPTION clause, so that users do not make a valid change that is outside the scope of their permissions.

8. *Display*. You have to CAST() every encoding for the front end. This can be a lot of overhead and a source of errors when the same monster string is CAST() to different data types in different programs.

5.3.5 Keep the Codes in the Database

A part of the database should have all of the codes stored in tables. These tables can be used to validate input, to translate codes in displays, and as part of the system documentation.

I was amazed to go to a major hospital in Los Angeles in mid-1993 and see the clerk still looking up codes in a dog-eared looseleaf notebook instead of bringing them up on her terminal screen. The hospital was still using an old IBM mainframe system, which had dumb 3270 terminals, rather than a client/server system with workstations. There was not even a help screen available to the clerk.

The translation tables can be downloaded to the workstations in a client/server system to reduce network traffic. They can also be used to build picklists on interactive screens and thereby reduce typographical errors. Changes to the codes are thereby propagated in the system without anyone having to rewrite application code. If the codes change over time, the table for a code should have to include a pair of "date effective" fields. This will allow a data warehouse to correctly read and translate old data.

5.4 Multiple Character Sets

Some DBMS products can support ASCII, EBCDIC, and Unicode. You need to be aware of this, so you can set proper collations and normalize your text.

The predicate "<string> IS [NOT] NORMALIZED" in SQL-99 determines if a Unicode string is one of four normal forms (i.e., D, C, KD, and KC). The use of the words *normal form* here is not the same as in a relational context. In the Unicode model, a single character can be built from several other characters. Accent marks can be put on basic Latin letters. Certain combinations of letters can be displayed as ligatures (ae becomes æ). Some languages, such as Hangul (Korean) and Vietnamese, build glyphs from concatenating symbols in two dimensions. Some languages have special forms of one letter that are determined by context, such as the terminal sigma in Greek or accented u in Czech. In short, writing is more complex than putting one letter after another.

The Unicode standard defines the order of such constructions in their normal forms. You can still produce the same results with different orderings and sometimes with different combinations of symbols, but it is handy when you are searching such text to know that it is normalized rather than trying to parse each glyph on the fly. You can find details about normalization and links to free software at www.unicode.org.

Coding Choices

"Caesar: Pardon him, Theodotus. He is a barbarian and thinks the customs of his tribe and island are the laws of nature."
—*Caesar and Cleopatra*, by George Bernard Shaw, 1898

THIS CHAPTER DEALS WITH writing good DML statements in Standard SQL. That means they are portable and can be optimized well by most SQL dialects. I define *portable* to mean one of several things. The code is standard and can be run as-is on other SQL dialects; standard implies portable. Or the code can be converted to another SQL dialect in a simple mechanical fashion, or that the feature used is so universal that all or most products have it in some form; portable does not imply standard. You can get some help with this concept from the X/Open SQL Portability Guides.

A major problem in becoming a SQL programmer is that people do not unlearn procedural or OO programming they had to learn for their first languages. They do not learn how to think in terms of sets and predicates, and so they mimic the solutions they know in their first programming languages. Jerry Weinberg (1978) observed this fact more than 25 years ago in his classic book, *Psychology of Computer Programming*. He was teaching PL/I. For those of you younger readers, PL/I was a language from IBM that was a hybrid of FORTRAN, COBOL, and AlGOL that had a popular craze.

Weinberg found that he could tell the first programming languages of the students by how they wrote PL/I. My personal experience (1989) was that I could guess the nationality of the students in my C and Pascal programming classes because of their native spoken language.

Another problem in becoming a SQL programmer is that people tend to become SQL dialect programmers and think that their particular product's SQL is some kind of standard. In 2004, I had a job interview for a position where I was being asked to evaluate different platforms for a major size increase in the company's databases. The interviewer kept asking me "general SQL" questions based on the storage architecture of the only product he knew.

His product is not intended for Very Large Database (VLDB) applications, and he had no knowledge of Nucleus, Teradata, Model 204, or other products that compete in the VLDB arena. He had spent his career tuning one version of one product and could not make the jump to anything different, even conceptually. His career is about to become endangered.

There is a place for the specialist dialect programmer, but dialect programming should be a last resort in special circumstances and never the first attempt. Think of it as cancer surgery: You do massive surgery when there is a bad tumor that is not treatable by other means; you do not start with it when the patient came in with acne.

6.1 Pick Standard Constructions over Proprietary Constructions

There is a fact of life in the IT industry called the Code Museum Effect, which works like this: First, each vendor adds a feature to its product. The feature is deemed useful, so it gets into the next version of the standard with slightly different syntax or semantics, but the vendor is stuck with its proprietary syntax. Its users have written code based on it, and they do not want to redo it. The solutions are the following:

1. *Never implement the standard and just retain the old syntax*. The problem is that you cannot pass a conformance test, which can be required for government and industry contracts. SQL programmers who know the standard from other products cannot read, write, or maintain your code easily. In short, you have the database equivalent of last year's cell phone.

2. *Implement the standard, but retain the old syntax, too*. This is the usual solution for a few releases. It gives the users a chance to

move to the standard syntax but does not break the existing applications. Everyone is happy for awhile.

3. *Implement the standard and depreciate the old syntax*. The vendor is ready for a major release, which lets it redo major parts of the database engine. Changing to the standard syntax and not supporting the old syntax at this point is a good way to force users to upgrade their software and help pay for that major release.

A professional programmer would be converting his or her old code at step two to avoid being trapped in the Code Museum when step three rolls around. Let's be honest, massive code conversions do not happen until after step three occurs in most shops, and they are a mess, but you can start to avoid the problems by always writing standard code in a step two situation.

6.1.1 Use Standard OUTER JOIN Syntax

Rationale:
Here is how the standard OUTER JOINs work in SQL-92. Assume you are given:

```
Table1        Table2
 a   b         a   c
 ======        ======
 1   w         1   r
 2   x         2   s
 3   y         3   t
 4   z
```

and the OUTER JOIN expression:

```
Table1
LEFT OUTER JOIN
Table2
ON Table1.a = Table2.a          <== join condition
   AND Table2.c = 't';          <== single table condition
```

We call Table1 the "preserved table" and Table2 the "unpreserved table" in the query. What I am going to give you is a little different but equivalent to the ANSI/ISO standards.

1. We build the CROSS JOIN of the two tables. Scan each row in the result set.
2. If the predicate tests TRUE for that row, then you keep it. You also remove all rows derived from it from the CROSS JOIN.
3. If the predicate tests FALSE or UNKNOWN for that row, then keep the columns from the preserved table, convert all the columns from the unpreserved table to NULLs, and remove the duplicates.

So let us execute this by hand:

```
Let @ = passed the first predicate
Let * = passed the second predicate
```

Table1 CROSS JOIN Table2

```
a   b       a   c
=========================
1   w       1   r @
1   w       2   s
1   w       3   t *
2   x       1   r
2   x       2   s @
2   x       3   t *
3   y       1   r
3   y       2   s
3   y       3   t @* <== the TRUE set
4   z       1   r
4   z       2   s
4   z       3   t *
```

Table1 LEFT OUTER JOIN Table2

```
a   b       a   c
=========================
3   y     3      t      <= only TRUE row
-----------------------
1   w     NULL  NULL  Sets of duplicates
1   w     NULL  NULL
1   w     NULL  NULL
```

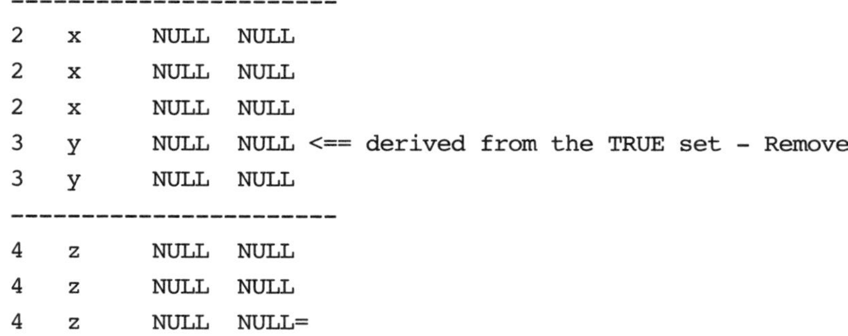

```
-----------------------
2   x     NULL  NULL
2   x     NULL  NULL
2   x     NULL  NULL
3   y     NULL  NULL <== derived from the TRUE set - Remove
3   y     NULL  NULL
-----------------------
4   z     NULL  NULL
4   z     NULL  NULL
4   z     NULL  NULL=
```

The final results:

```
Table1 LEFT OUTER JOIN Table2
a   b         a   c
=========================
1   w     NULL  NULL
2   x     NULL  NULL
3   y     3      t
4   z     NULL  NULL
```

The basic rule is that every row in the preserved table is represented in the results in at least one result row.

6.1.1.1 Extended Equality and Proprietary Syntax

Before the standard was set, vendors all had a slightly different syntax with slightly different semantics. Most of them involved an extended equality operator based on the original Sybase implementation. There are limitations and serious problems with the extended equality, however. Consider the two Chris Date tables:

```
Suppliers          SupParts
supno               supno partno qty
=========          ==============
S1                 S1    P1     100
S2                 S1    P2     250
S3                 S2    P1     100
                   S2    P2     250
```

And let's do a Sybase-style extended equality OUTER JOIN like this:

```
SELECT *
 FROM Supplier, SupParts
WHERE Supplier.supno *= SupParts.supno
  AND qty < 200;
```

If I do the OUTER join first, I get:

```
Suppliers LOJ SupParts
supno supno partno qty
=======================
S1      S1   P1     100
S1      S1   P2     250
S2      S2   P1     100
S2      S2   P2     250
S3    NULL NULL    NULL
```

Then I apply the (qty < 200) predicate and get:

```
Suppliers LOJ SupParts
supno supno partno qty
===================
S1   S1   P1    100
S2   S2   P1    100
```

Doing it in the opposite order results in the following:

```
Suppliers LOJ SupParts
supno supno partno qty
===================
S1   S1   P1    100
S2   S2   P1    100
S3   NULL NULL NULL
```

Sybase does it one way, Oracle does it another, and Centura (née Gupta) lets you pick which one to use—the worst of both nonstandard worlds! In SQL-92, you have a choice and can force the order of execution. Either do the predicates after the join:

```
SELECT *
  FROM Supplier
       LEFT OUTER JOIN
       SupParts
       ON Supplier.supno = SupParts.supno
WHERE qty < 200;
```

or do it in the joining:

```
SELECT *
 FROM Supplier
      LEFT OUTER JOIN
      SupParts
      ON Supplier.supno = SupParts.supno
         AND qty < 200;
```

Another problem is that you cannot show the same table as preserved and unpreserved in the extended equality version, but it is easy in SQL-92. For example, to find the students who have taken Math 101 and might have taken Math 102:

```
SELECT C1.student, C1.math, C2.math
 FROM (SELECT * FROM Courses WHERE math = 101) AS C1
      LEFT OUTER JOIN
      (SELECT * FROM Courses WHERE math = 102) AS C2
      ON C1.student = C2.student;
```

Exceptions:
None. Almost every vendor, major and minor, has the ANSI infixed OUTER JOIN operator today. You will see various proprietary notations in legacy code, and you can convert it by following the discussion given previously.

6.1.2 Infixed INNER JOIN and CROSS JOIN Syntax Is Optional, but Nice

SQL-92 introduced the INNER JOIN and CROSS JOIN operators to match the OUTER JOIN operators and complete the notation; other infixed JOIN operators are not widely implemented but exist for completeness. The functionality of the INNER JOIN and CROSS JOIN

existed in the FROM clause before and did not give the programmer anything new like the OUTER JOINs.

Rationale:

The CROSS JOIN is a handy piece of documentation that is much harder to miss seeing than a simple comma. Likewise, writing out INNER JOIN instead of the shorthand INNER helps document the code.

However, many INNER JOIN operators can be visually confusing, and you might consider using the older syntax. The older syntax lets you put all of the predicates in one place and group them in some manner for readability. A rule of thumb is the "rule of five" in human psychology. This says that we have problems handling more than five things at once, get serious problems with seven, and break down at nine (Miller 1956).

So when you have fewer than five tables, the infixed operators are fine but questionable for more than five INNER JOIN-ed tables. Trying to associate ON clauses to INNER JOIN operators is visually difficult. In particular, a Star Schema has an easily recognized pattern of joins from the fact table to each dimension table, like this in pseudocode:

```
 SELECT ..
   FROM Facts, Dim1, Dim2, .., DimN
WHERE Facts.a1 = Dim1.a
  AND Facts.a2 = Dim2.a
  ..
  AND Facts.an = DimN.a
```

The reader can look down the right-hand side of the WHERE clause and see the dimensions in a vertical list.

One style that is popular is to put the join conditions in the FROM clause with INNER JOIN syntax, then do the search arguments in the WHERE clause. Some newbies believe that this is required, but it is not. However, if the search arguments change, having them in one place is handy.

A quick heuristic when using old-style joins is that the number of tables in the FROM clause should be one more than the number of join conditions in the WHERE clause. This shows that you do not have cycles in the joins. If the difference between the number of tables and the number of join conditions is more than one, then you might have an unwanted CROSS JOIN caused by a missing join condition.

Old style:

```
SELECT O1.order_nbr, ..
  FROM Orders AS O1,
       OrderDetails AS D1
 WHERE O1.order_nbr = D1.order_nbr
   AND D1.dept = 'mens wear';
```

New style:

```
SELECT O1.order_nbr, ..
  FROM Orders AS O1
       INNER JOIN
       OrderDetails AS D1
       ON O1.order_nbr = D1.order_nbr
          AND D1.dept = 'mens wear';
```

Mixed style:

```
SELECT O1.order_nbr, ..
  FROM Orders AS O1
       INNER JOIN
       OrderDetails AS D1
       ON O1.order_nbr = D1.order_nbr
 WHERE D1.dept = 'mens wear';
```

Exceptions:

The infixed join operators must be used if there is an OUTER JOIN in the FROM clause. The reason is that the order of execution matters with OUTER JOINs, and you can control it better with parentheses and predicates if they are all together.

As a rule of thumb, when you have a FROM clause with five or more tables in it, the traditional syntax is probably easier to read than trying to visually match the ON clauses to the proper tables and correlation names. This rule of five is mentioned in other places as a limit on human data processing ability.

6.1.3 Use ISO Temporal Syntax

Rationale:

The only display format allowed for temporal data in Standard SQL is based on ISO-8601, and it is the "yyyy-mm-dd hh:mm:ss.sssss" style. The Federal Information Processing Standards (FIPS) require at least five decimal places of precision in the seconds. Anything else is ambiguous

and not acceptable if you want to work with other software that follows ISO standards.

Standard SQL defines a minimal set of simple temporal math operators. All of them are available in all SQL products, but the syntax varies. For example, in the T-SQL dialect, the function call "DATEADD (DD, 13, birthdate)" adds "13" days to the date in birthdate. The Standard SQL syntax for the same calculation is "birthdate + INTERVAL '13' DAY" instead.

You can set the display to ISO-8601 in every SQL product, and you can do 99.99 percent of your temporal work without any proprietary temporal functions. The problem is that porting code can be a bother. You need to make a set of notes about any differences in your dialect and the standard.

Exceptions:

None. Display formatting is always done in the client layer of a tiered architecture. This is a basic programming principle and has nothing to do with SQL per se. Failure to follow this principle is usually the result of a newbie who came to SQL from a traditional monolithic language with a strong coupling between the application, the display, and the file system.

6.1.4 Use Standard and Portable Functions

Rationale:

Standard SQL is not a computational language, so it does not have the function library of FORTRAN or a statistical package. SQL is not a text manipulation language, so it does not have the function library of ICON or Snobol. All you have is simple four-function math and basic string operators in SQL-92. Vendors have always provided more than just the basic operators, so you can write portable code that assumes other math and string functions. The most common extra math functions are modulus, rounding and truncation, powers, and logarithms. The most extra common string functions are replacement, reversal, and repetition.

Exceptions:

If your dialect has a function built into it, which would require a huge amount of code to implement or a really long running time, then use the proprietary function and comment it for porting.

6.2 Pick Compact Constructions over Longer Equivalents

"Entia non sunt multiplicanda praeter necessitatem." (*No more things should be presumed to exist than are absolutely necessary.*)
—William Occam (c. 1280–1349).

"Everything should be made as simple as possible, but not simpler."
—Attributed to Albert Einstein

Writing code in as short, clear, and compact a form as possible is just good software engineering for any programming language. Modules that clearly do one function are easier to modify and to understand. Systems with fewer modules are easier to maintain.

SQL can replace hundreds of lines of procedural code with a few statements. You ought to be predisposed to think of short, clean solutions instead of kludges. However, old habits are hard to kill. Many newbies still think in terms of logical tests based on Boolean logic and simple AND-OR-NOT expressions that they know from their first programming languages.

6.2.1 Avoid Extra Parentheses

Rationale:

Newbies see generated SQL code that has to have extra levels of parentheses to execute safely and think that this is the way to write code. Consider this simple query:

```
SELECT a, b, c
  FROM Foobar
 WHERE (a = b)
   AND (c < 42);
```

This is not so bad to read, but by the time you have more than five predicates and useless nesting of parentheses, the code is difficult to read, and a missing parentheses is a real pain to locate. Let LISP programmers use them; they really need parentheses.

Exceptions:

Parentheses in moderation can make nested predicates easier to read:

```
SELECT application_nbr
  FROM LoanApplications
 WHERE years_employed > 5 OR net_worth > loan_amt
       AND monthly_expenses < 0.25 * loan_amt
       OR collateral > 2.00 * loan_amt AND age > 25
       OR collateral > loan_amt AND age > 30
       OR years_employed > 2 AND net_worth > 2.00 * loan_amt
       AND Age > 21 AND monthly_expenses < 0.50 * loan_amt;
```

versus:

```
SELECT application_nbr
  FROM LoanApplications
 WHERE years_employed > 5
    OR (net_worth > loan_amt
        AND monthly_expenses < 0.25 * loan_amt)
    OR (collateral > 2.00 * loan_amt AND age > 25)
    OR (collateral > loan_amt AND age > 30)
    OR (years_employed > 2
        AND net_worth > 2.00 * loan_amt
        AND age > 21
        AND monthly_expenses < 0.50 * loan_amt);
```

In the following section, we will also see how to use a CASE expression for situations like this one.

6.2.2 Use CASE Family Expressions

The CASE expression is an expression and not a control statement; that is, it returns a value of one data type. Because SQL is declarative, there is no flow of control for it to modify, like the CASE statements in other languages. The number of newbies who do not understand the difference between an expression and a statement is frightening.

The idea and the syntax came from the ADA programming language. Here is the formal BNF syntax for a <case specification>:

```
<case specification> ::= <simple case> | <searched case>

<simple case> ::=
   CASE <case operand>
     <simple when clause>...
     [<else clause>]
   END
```

```
<searched case> ::=
   CASE
     <searched when clause>...
     [<else clause>]
   END

<simple when clause> ::= WHEN <when operand> THEN <result>

<searched when clause> ::= WHEN <search condition> THEN
<result>

<else clause> ::= ELSE <result>

<case operand> ::= <value expression>

<when operand> ::= <value expression>

<result> ::= <result expression> | NULL

<result expression> ::= <value expression>
```

6.2.2.1 Searched CASE Expression

The searched CASE expression is probably the most-used version of the expression. The WHEN ... THEN ... clauses are executed in left-to-right order. The first WHEN clause that tests TRUE returns the value given in its THEN clause, and you can nest CASE expressions inside of each other. If no explicit ELSE clause is given for the CASE expression, then the database will insert an implicit "ELSE NULL" clause. If you want to return a NULL in a THEN clause, you must use a CAST (NULL AS <datatype>) expression. I recommend always giving the ELSE clause, so that you can change it later when you find something explicit to return.

6.2.2.2 Simple CASE Expression

The <simple case expression> is defined as a searched CASE expression in which all of the WHEN clauses are made into equality comparisons against the <case operand>. For example:

```
CASE iso_sex_code
WHEN 0 THEN 'Unknown'
WHEN 1 THEN 'Male'
WHEN 2 THEN 'Female'
```

```
WHEN 9 THEN 'N/A'
ELSE NULL END
```

could also be written as:

```
CASE
WHEN iso_sex_code = 0 THEN 'Unknown'
WHEN iso_sex_code = 1 THEN 'Male'
WHEN iso_sex_code = 2 THEN 'Female'
WHEN iso_sex_code = 9 THEN 'N/A'
ELSE NULL END
```

There is a gimmick in this definition, however. The expression:

```
CASE foo
WHEN 1 THEN 'bar'
WHEN NULL THEN 'no bar'
END
```

becomes:

```
CASE WHEN foo = 1 THEN 'bar'
     WHEN foo = NULL THEN 'no_bar' —error!
     ELSE NULL END
```

The second WHEN clause is always UNKNOWN. Use the simple CASE expression when it is appropriate.

6.2.2.3 Other CASE Expressions

The SQL-92 standard defines other functions in terms of the CASE expression, which makes the language a bit more compact and easier to implement. For example, the COALESCE () function can be defined for one or two expressions by:

1. COALESCE (<value exp #1>) is equivalent to (<value exp #1>)
2. COALESCE (<value exp #1>, <value exp #2>) is equivalent to:

```
CASE WHEN <value exp #1> IS NOT NULL
     THEN <value exp #1>
     ELSE <value exp #2> END
```

Then we can recursively define it for (*n*) expressions, where (*n* >= 3), in the list by:

COALESCE (<value exp #1>, <value exp #2>, ..., *n*) as equivalent to:

```
CASE WHEN <value exp #1> IS NOT NULL
     THEN <value exp #1>
     ELSE COALESCE (<value exp #2>, ..., n)
END
```

Likewise, NULLIF (<value exp #1>, <value exp #2>) is equivalent to:

```
CASE WHEN <value exp #1> = <value exp #2>
     THEN NULL
     ELSE <value exp #1> END
```

Use the most compact form of these CASE expressions, and do not expand them out to their definitions.

6.2.3 Avoid Redundant Expressions

Rationale:

Most modern SQL engines are pretty smart. This was not always the case, so older SQL programmers will sometimes add redundant predicates to a where clause. For example, if none of the columns in the table Foobar is NULL-able, then given:

```
SELECT a, b, c
  FROM Foobar
WHERE a = b
  AND b = c
  AND c = a;
```

One of the three search conditions is redundant, because it can be deduced from the other two. Redundant predicates only confuse the human readers and do not give information to a good optimizer.

Exceptions:
If your SQL has a bad optimizer and needs the extra help, then add redundant predicates.

6.2.4 Seek a Compact Form

Rationale:
Many of the earlier SQL engines could not use an index on a column if it were in an expression, and they did not do any algebraic optimizations. Today, we do this bit of cleanup work because a simpler form of an expression is easier to maintain and to read:

```
SELECT a, b, c
  FROM Foobar
WHERE a + 2 = b - 4;
```

And a little algebra becomes:

```
SELECT a, b, c
  FROM Foobar
 WHERE a = b + 2;
```

Exceptions:
If your SQL has a really good optimizer, and the complicated form is easier for a human being to read for some reason, then use it. Sometimes there is no simple form.

6.2.4.1 Use BETWEEN, Not AND-ed Predicates

Rationale:
Consider this simple query:

```
SELECT a, b, c
  FROM Foobar
WHERE a <= b
  AND b <= c;
```

which can be written as:

```
SELECT a, b, c
  FROM Foobar
 WHERE b BETWEEN a AND c;
```

The BETWEEN is more compact and gives the reader information about the relationship among three columns that might not be so obvious amid a longer list of search conditions.

Exceptions:
This rule makes sense from a readability standpoint, but it does not always stand up in terms of performance. Consider DB2 for z/OS in which "<column name> BETWEEN <expression> AND <expression> is both indexable and a stage one predicate." Without explaining what a stage one predicate is, it is preferred for performance.

However, "<value> BETWEEN <column name 1>AND <column name 2>" is both stage two and nonindexable, but formulating the same using two <= predicates could be both stage one and indexable and therefore preferable for performance. Likewise, the same execution plan applies to "<column name 1> BETWEEN <column name 2> AND <column name 3>" predicates. This will differ from DBMS to DBMS and platform to platform. As optimizers get better, this will be less and less true.

6.2.4.2 Use IN(), Not OR-ed predicates

Rationale:
The IN() predicate was first introduced in the Pascal programming language. In SQL it has two forms; the list and the subquery. The list form has a comma-separated list of values or expressions on the right-hand side. The predicate returns a TRUE result if there is a match in that list with the left-hand side of the predicate. It is shorthand for a list or OR-ed predicates. For example consider:

```
SELECT a, b, c
  FROM Foobar
WHERE a = b
   OR a = c;
```

which can be written as:

```
SELECT a, b, c
  FROM Foobar
WHERE a IN (b, c);
```

The IN() is more compact and gives the reader information about the relationship among three columns that might not be so obvious amid a

longer list of search conditions. The list can also consist of scalar expressions, but that is not common.

Exceptions:
Watch out for NULLs! The IN () predicate is defined as a chain of OR-ed predicates, thus:

```
a IN (x, y, z)
means ((a = x) OR (a = y) OR (a = z))
```

Therefore:

```
a IN (x, y, NULL)
means ((a = x) OR (a = y) OR (a = NULL))
      ((a = x) OR (a = y) OR UNKNOWN)
```

We are now in SQL's three-valued logic. Remember that a NULL is not the same thing as an UNKNOWN; SQL-92 has no Boolean data type; and you cannot use AND, OR, and NOT on a NULL.

The NOT IN () predicate is defined as the negation of the IN():

```
a NOT IN (x, y, z)
```

means:

```
NOT (a IN (x, y, z))
      NOT ((a = x) OR (a = y) OR (a = z))
      (NOT(a = x) AND NOT(a = y) AND NOT(a = z)) --DeMorgan's law
      ((a <> x) AND (a <> y) AND (a <> z)) --definition
```

Now put in a NULL for one of the list elements:

```
((a <> x) AND (a <> y) AND UNKNOWN)
(UNKNOWN)
```

If you wish to have a match on a NULL in a list, then you can COALESCE() the NULLs to the left-hand expression, thus:

```
 WHERE a IN (x, y, COALESCE (z, a))
```

which is a little cleaner than:

```
WHERE (a IN (x, y) OR z IS NULL)
```

6.2.4.3 Use CASE Expressions, Not Complex Nested Predicates

An advanced trick in the WHERE clause is to use a CASE expression for a complex predicate with material implications. If you forgot your freshman logic, a material implication logical operator is written as an arrow with two tails, and it means "p implies q" or "if p is true then q is true" in English.

```
WHERE CASE
      WHEN <search condition #1>
      THEN 1
      WHEN <search condition #2>
      THEN 1
       ...
      ELSE 0 END = 1
```

The use of a function that returns one or zero when given a predicate as its parameter is called a *characteristic function* in logic and set theory.

Review the rules for the CASE expression in section 6.2.2 first, so you understand it. The order of execution of the WHEN clauses can be used to optimize performance and avoid redundant tests. You can also nest CASE expressions inside the WHEN and THEN clauses of a containing CASE expression and display the logic as an indented tree structure.

```
WHERE CASE
      WHEN <search condition #1>
      THEN CASE
           WHEN <search condition #1.1>
           THEN 1
           WHEN <search condition #1.2>
           THEN 1 ELSE 0 END
      WHEN <search condition #2>
      THEN 1
       ...
      ELSE 0 END = 1
```

The goal of this technique is to replace pages of long lists of simple theta expressions inside horrible levels of parentheses and to provide

some short-circuit evaluation as a bonus. When the nesting is too messy to understand, stop and reconsider your logic. Decision table tools, such as Logic Gem, are an excellent way to do this.

6.3 Use Comments

Rationale:

The best documentation for maintaining a program has been comments in the code. Perhaps it is easier for procedural language programmers to add comments because they are explaining in a narrative fashion what their program is doing. Unfortunately, procedural language comments are often redundant if you can read the code. How much help did you get from:

```
UPDATE Teams
   SET score = score + 1;—increment score
```

which gives you no information about what the variable score means and why it is incremented.

In Standard SQL, a comment begins with two dashes (--) and ends with a new line, because the first SQL engines were on IBM mainframes and used punchcards. This format is a poor choice with modern computers that can store free-form text. Word wrap in program text can split a comment and give you errors. Because SQL supports the unary minus operator, this is ambiguous in some rare situations and makes the compiler work extra hard. Later standards added the C style /* and */ pairs, and many vendors have similar comment brackets. They are a better choice.

SQL programmers do not like to put comments in their code, not even redundant or useless ones. My guess is that because SQL does a lot of work in one statement and programmers have been taught to comment the code at the statement execution level rather than explain the purpose of the code, the higher level of abstraction confuses them. They are not inclined to put comments at the clause level because the appearance of the code can be crowded.

Get over it. You need a high-level descriptive comment on a block of SQL, and then more detailed comments on a few important clauses. Try to keep the comments aimed at non-SQL programmers and in plain English. For example, don't say "relational division of motor pool vehicles by available drivers" on the assumption that the reader will know what a relational division is. Try "list all drivers who can drive all the vehicles in the motor pool" instead. The other trick is to reference the documentation for the schema and the applications. This assumes that they are current and useful, however.

If you have the time, another guru-level trick is to save the best of the various statements you tried that worked but did not perform as well as the final choice as comments. In SQL, what was the best answer in one situation is often no longer the best answer. Instead of making the next programmer start from scratch, share your notes.

Exceptions:
In a well-designed schema with good data element names, much of the code is easy for an experienced SQL programmer to read. You can skip comments on single statements if their intent is really obvious, but remember that one programmer's obvious is another's "what the heck?" when you code.

6.3.1 Stored Procedures

Always start a stored procedure with a comment that gives at least the author, the date, and the update history. This is simply basic software management. After that, add a high-level description of the function of this module. The procedure name will be in a "<verb><object>" format. Each parameter should have a comment as needed.

6.3.2 Control Statement Comments

Comments on control statements, such as IF-THEN-ELSE, BEGIN-END, and WHILE-DO loops, will look much like comments in any procedural program. Complicated SQL statements need a comment at the top and often comments at the clause level.

6.3.3 Comments on Clause

This point is difficult to generalize, but things that act as a unit might need a comment. For example, a derived table for which there is no good alias might need a comment to explain what it contains. A series of predicates that define a complicated join might be prefaced with a comment to explain what they are doing at a higher level.

6.4 Avoid Optimizer Hints

Rationale:

Many products have proprietary syntax for sending parameters to the optimizer to change the execution plan for a statement. Because each physical implementation is different, this syntax will not be portable, but there are other problems too.

First, the optimizer is usually smarter than the programmer and finds a good plan. People cannot handle computations that involve tens of parameters very well. Second, once a hint is put on a statement, it stays there permanently, long after the reason for the hint is gone. A typical example of this would set up a query hint for a skewed statistical distribution and then, as the database grows, the distribution becomes more normal or skewed in the opposite direction. The hint that used to be so helpful is now a handicap.

Exceptions:

If you do have a skewed statistical distribution or other weirdness in your data that is destroying performance, then use a hint. Set up a review of all statements with hints to see if they actually need to be maintained. Reviews should occur when a new release of database is installed (optimizer might be better) or the statistics of one or more of the tables change (data might be better), but if the performance is acceptable, then do not use hints.

6.5 Avoid Triggers in Favor of DRI Actions

Rationale:

Although there is an ANSI/ISO standard for triggers, their syntax and semantics are still highly proprietary. Triggers are blocks of procedural code that are executed (fired) when a database event occurs to a table. This code is usually in a proprietary 3GL language. A database event is something that changes the data—an insert, update, or delete.

The full ANSI version of triggers does not fire on an insertion, but some vendor products do. The full ANSI version of triggers have more than one trigger on a table and can fire them in a sequence either before or after the database event. Most vendor products do not have that much control over the triggers. On the other hand, the syntax and semantics for DRI actions are well defined and standardized.

A newbie posted a topic under the title "Need Help with a Calculation Trigger" on the forums in the SQL Server Central Web site in November 2004. This person was having trouble setting up a trigger to check the units of a "number field [sic]"; the real problem was that the poster did not know that a column is not a field.

For some reason, the column was declared as FLOAT and was called length. The trouble is that some people were entering a length in meters, centimeters, and millimeters. The poster was trying to code a trigger that will fire on UPDATE or INSERT to check the value of length. If it is greater than 20, chances are the number is in millimeters and should be divided by 10. If the number is less than 0, then the number is probably in meters and should be multiplied by 100.

```
CREATE TRIGGER SetCentimeters
AFTER INSERT ON Samples
UPDATE Samples
   SET length
       = (CASE
          WHEN length > 10.00
          THEN Length / 10.00
          WHEN length < 0.00
          THEN Length * 100.00
          ELSE Length END)
 WHERE length NOT BETWEEN 0.00 AND 10.00;
```

However, this is the wrong answer. It is in procedural code. The right answer is in the DDL, with something like this:

```
length DECIMAL(2,1) NOT NULL
       CONSTRAINT length_in_centimeters_only
       CHECK (length BETWEEN 0.01 AND 9.99)
```

Triggers tend to fix errors on the fly; the goal is not to permit them in the first place.

Exceptions:

Some things should be done with triggers because you cannot do them with DRI. In particular, the INSTEAD OF trigger has to be used for updatable views. This trigger is attached to a VIEW, and instead of taking actions on the VIEW, it changes the base tables from which the VIEW is built, so that the user sees those changes reflected in the VIEW.

Heuristics tend to favor stored procedures over triggers. A trigger fires every time its database event occurs, which puts it out of your control and adds that overhead to each database event. A stored

procedure has to be deliberately executed, which puts it completely in your control. Furthermore, the syntax for triggers is proprietary despite the standards, so they do not port well.

6.6 Use SQL Stored Procedures

Every SQL product has some kind of 4GL language that allows you to write stored procedures that reside in the database and that can be invoked from a host program. Although there is a SQL/PSM standard, in the real world, only Mimer and IBM have implemented it at the time of this writing. Instead, each vendor has a proprietary 4GL, such as T-SQL for the Sybase/SQL Server family, PL/SQL from Oracle, Informix-4GL from Informix, and so forth. For more details on these languages, I recommend that you get a copy of Jim Melton's excellent book, *Understanding SQL's Stored Procedures* ISBN: 1-55860461-8 [out of print] on the subject. The advantages they have are considerable, including the following:

- *Security*. The users can only do what the stored procedure allows them to do, whereas dynamic SQL or other ad hoc access to the database allows them to do anything to the database. The safety and security issues ought to be obvious.
- *Maintenance*. The stored procedure can be easily replaced and recompiled with an improved version. All of the host language programs that call it will benefit from the improvements that were made and not be aware of the change.
- *Network traffic*. Because only parameters are passed, network traffic is lower than passing SQL code to the database across the network.
- *Consistency*. If a task is always done with a stored procedure, then it will be done the same way each time. Otherwise, you have to depend on all programmers (present and future) getting it right. Programmers are not evil, but they are human. When you tell someone that a customer has to be at least 18 years of age, one programmer will code "age > 18" and another will code "age >= 18" without any evil intent. You cannot expect everyone to remember all of the business rules and write flawless code forever.
- *Modularity*. Once you have a library of stored procedures, you can reuse them to build other procedures. Why reinvent the wheel every week?

Chapter 8 is a general look at how to write stored procedures in SQL. If you look at any of the SQL newsgroups, you will see awful code. Apparently, programmers are not taking a basic software engineering course anymore, or they think that the old rules do not apply to a vendor's 4GL language.

6.7 Avoid User-Defined Functions and Extensions inside the Database

Rationale:

SQL is a set-oriented language and wants to work with tables rather than scalars, but programmers will try to get around this model of programming to return to what they know by writing user-defined functions in other languages and putting them into the database.

There are two kinds of user-defined functions and extensions. Some SQL products allow functions written in another standard language to become part of the database and to be used as if they were just another part of SQL. Others have a proprietary language in the database that allows the user to write extensions.

Even the SQL/PSM allows you to write user-defined functions in any of the ANSI X3J standard programming languages that have data-type conversions and interfaces defined for SQL. There is a LANGUAGE clause in the CREATE PROCEDURE statement for this purpose.

Microsoft has its common language runtime (CLR), which takes this one step further and embeds code from any compiler that can produce a CLR module in its SQL Server. Illustra's "data blade" technology is now part of Informix, IBM has "extenders" to add functionality to the basic RDBMS, and Oracle has various "Cartridges" for its product.

The rationale behind all of these various user-defined functions and extensions is to make the vendor's product more powerful and to avoid having to get another package for nontraditional data, such as temporal and spatial information. However, user-defined functions are difficult to maintain, destroy portability, and can affect data integrity.

Exceptions:

You might have a problem that can be solved with such tools, but this is a rare event in most cases; most data processing applications can be done just fine with standard SQL. You need to justify such a decision and be ready to do the extra work required.

6.7.1 Multiple Language Problems

Programming languages do not work the same way, so by allowing multiple languages to operate inside the database, you can lose data integrity. Just as quick examples: How does your language compare strings? The Xbase family ignores case and truncates the longer string, whereas SQL pads the shorter string and is case sensitive. How does your language handle a MOD() function when one or both arguments are negative? How does your language handle rounding and truncation? By hiding the fact that there is an interface between the SQL and the 3GL, you hide the problems without solving them.

6.7.2 Portability Problems

The proprietary user-defined functions and extensions will not port to another product, so you are locking yourself into one vendor. It is also difficult to find programmers who are proficient in several languages to even maintain the code, much less port it.

6.7.3 Optimization Problems

The code from a user-defined function is not integrated into the compiler. It has to be executed by itself when it appears in an expression. As a simple example of this principle, most compilers can do algebraic simplifications, because they know about the standard functions. They cannot do this with user-defined functions for fear of side effects. Also, 3GL languages are not designed to work on tables. You have to call them on each row level, which can be costly.

6.8 Avoid Excessive Secondary Indexes

First, not all SQL products use indexes: Nucleus is based on a compressed bit vector, Teradata uses hashing, and so forth. However, tree-structured indexes of various kinds are common enough to be worth mentioning. The X/Open SQL Portability Guides give a basic syntax that is close to that used in various dialects with minor embellishments. The user may or may not have control over the kind of index the system builds.

A primary index is an index created to enforce PRIMARY KEY and UNIQUE constraints in the database. Without them, your schema is simply not a correct data model, because no table would have a key.

A secondary index is an optional index created by the DBA to improve performance. The schema will return the same answers as it does with them, but perhaps not in a timely fashion—or even within the memory of living humans.

Indexes are one thing that the optimizer considers in building an execution plan. When and how the index is used depends on the kind of index, the query, and the statistical distribution of the data. A slight change to any of these could result in a new execution plan later. With that caveat, we can speak in general terms about tree-structured indexes.

If more than a certain percentage of a table is going to be used in a statement, then the indexes are ignored and the table is scanned from front to back. Using the index would involve more overhead than filtering the rows of the target table as they are read.

The fundamental problem is that redundant or unused indexes take up storage space and have to be maintained whenever their base tables are changed. They slow up every update, insert, or delete operation to the table. Although this event is rare, indexes can also fool the optimizer into making a bad decision. There are tools for particular SQL products that can suggest indexes based on the actual statements submitted to the SQL engine. Consider using one.

6.9 Avoid Correlated Subqueries

Rationale:

In the early days of SQL, the optimizers were not good at reducing complex SQL expressions that involved correlated subqueries. They would blindly execute loops inside loops, scanning the innermost tables repeatedly. The example used to illustrate this point was something like these two queries where "x" is not NULL-able and Table "Foo" is much larger than table "Bar," which produce the same results:

```
 SELECT a, b, c
   FROM Foo
  WHERE Foo.x
        IN (SELECT x FROM Bar);
```

versus

```
SELECT a, b, c
   FROM Foo
  WHERE EXISTS
        (SELECT *
           FROM Bar
          WHERE Foo.x = Bar.x;
```

In older SQL engines, the EXISTS() predicate would materialize a JOIN on the two tables and take longer. The IN() predicate would put the smaller table into main storage and scan it, perhaps sorting it to speed the search. This is not quite as true any more. Depending on the particular optimizer and the access method, correlated subqueries are not the monsters they once were. In fact, some products let you create indexes that prejoin tables, so they are the fastest way to execute such queries.

However, correlated subqueries are confusing to people to read, and not all optimizers are that smart yet. For example, consider a table that models loans and payments with a status code for each payment. This is a classic one-to-many relationship. The problem is to select the loans where all of the payments have a status code of 'F':

```
CREATE TABLE Loans
(loan_nbr INTEGER NOT NULL,
 payment_nbr INTEGER NOT NULL,
 payment_status CHAR(1) NOT NULL
   CHECK (payment_status IN ('F', 'U', 'S')),
PRIMARY KEY (loan_nbr, payment_nbr));
```

One answer to this problem uses this correlated scalar subquery in the SELECT list:

```
SELECT DISTINCT
       (SELECT loan_nbr
          FROM Loans AS L1
         GROUP BY L1.loan_nbr
        HAVING COUNT(L1.payment_status) = COUNT(L2.loan_nbr))
       AS parent
  FROM Loans AS L2
 WHERE L2.  payment_status = 'F'
 GROUP BY L2.loan_nbr;
```

This approach is backward. It works from the many side of the relationship to the one side, but with a little thought and starting from the one side, you can get this answer:

```
SELECT loan_nbr
  FROM Loans
 GROUP BY loan_nbr
```

```
HAVING MAX(payment_status) = 'F'
   AND MIN(payment_status) = 'F';
```

The self-reference and correlation are complicated for both humans and machines. Most optimizers are not smart enough to flatten the first query like this.

Exceptions:
If you have a problem that is easier to understand with correlated subqueries and your optimizer is good, then don't be so afraid of them.

6.10 Avoid UNIONs

Rationale:
UNIONs are usually not well optimized. Because they require that redundant duplicates be discarded, they force most SQL engines to do a sort before presenting the result set to the user. If possible, use UNION ALL instead. You should never have to build a chain of UNIONs from the same base table. That code can be written with OR-ed predicates or CASE expressions.

As an example of a horrible misuse of SQL, Chris White posted a procedure that built dynamic SQL that would then build a report. Aside from the obvious violations of basic software engineering, the output was so huge that it exceeded the text size limits of SQL Server. He was attempting to construct an entire report in the database by using UNIONs to get the 12 lines of the report in the right order, by assigning them a letter of the alphabet. The whole thing would take several pages to show, but it is an extraction of the printout lines that were constructed from just the General Ledger. I have not attempted to clean up much of the code, so there are many violations of good coding rules in this snippet.

```
. . .
UNION
SELECT DISTINCT 'J' AS section,
       'NUMBER CHECKS' AS description, '' AS branch,
       COUNT(DISTINCT GL.source) AS total1, 0 AS total2
   FROM GeneralLedger AS GL
  WHERE GL.period >= :start_period
    AND GL.period <= :end_period
    AND GL.year_for_period = :period_yr
```

```
    AND GL.account_number IN ('3020')
    AND GL.journal_id IN ('CD')
UNION
SELECT DISTINCT 'C' AS section,
       'CASH RECEIPTS' AS description, '' AS branch,
       SUM(GL.amount) * -1 AS total1, 0 AS total2
  FROM GeneralLedger AS GL
 WHERE GL.period >= :start_period
   AND GL.period <= :end_period
   AND GL.year_for_period = :period_yr
   AND GL.account_number = '1050'
   AND GL.journal_id IN ('CR')
UNION
SELECT DISTINCT 'D' AS section,
       'NUMBER INVOICES' AS description, '' AS branch,
       COUNT(DISTINCT GL.source) AS total1, 0 AS total2
  FROM GeneralLedger AS GL
WHERE GL.period >= :start_period
  AND GL.period <= :end_period
  AND GL.year_for_period = :period_yr
  AND GL.account_number IN ('6010', '6090')
  AND GL.journal_id IN ('SJ')
UNION
SELECT DISTINCT 'E' AS section,
       'VOUCHER TOTAL' AS description, '' AS branch,
       SUM(GL.amount) * -1 AS total1, 0 AS total2
 FROM GeneralLedger AS GL
WHERE GL.period >= :start_period
   AND GL.period <= :end_period
  AND GL.year_for_period = :period_yr
  AND GL.account_number = '3020'
  AND GL.journal_id IN ('PJ', 'TJ')
UNION
SELECT DISTINCT 'F' AS section,
       'CHECKS PRINTED' AS description, '' AS branch,
       SUM(GL.amount) AS total1, 0 AS total2
FROM GeneralLedger AS GL
WHERE GL.period >= :start_period
  AND GL.period <= :end_period
  AND GL.year_for_period = :period_yr
  AND GL.account_number IN ('3020')
```

```
  AND GL.journal_id IN ('CD')
UNION
SELECT DISTINCT 'K' AS section,
       'NUMBER VOUCHERS' AS description, '' AS branch,
       COUNT(DISTINCT GL.source) AS total1, 0 AS total2
  FROM GeneralLedger AS GL
 WHERE GL.period >= :start_period
   AND GL.period <= :end_period
   AND GL.year_for_period = :period_yr
   AND GL.account_number IN ('3020')
   AND GL.journal_id IN ('PJ', 'TJ');
```

The last part of the code could be reduced to a single, cohesive procedure. The output of the procedure would then be formatted in the front. Notice that section, description, and branch are all placeholders to give a slot for columns in the other UNIONs not shown here.

```
CREATE PROCEDURE GeneralLedgeSummary (start_period DATE,
end_period DATE)
SELECT
COUNT(DISTINCT CASE WHEN acct_nbr = '3020' AND journal_code =
'CD'
               THEN source ELSE NULL END),
-SUM(CASE WHEN acct_nbr = '1050' AND journal_code ='CR'
     THEN amount ELSE 0.00 END),
COUNT(DISTINCT CASE WHEN acct_nbr IN ('6010', '6090') AND
journal_code = 'SJ'
               THEN source ELSE NULL END),
-SUM(CASE WHEN acct_nbr = '1050' AND journal_code = 'CR'
     THEN amount ELSE 0.00 END),
SUM(CASE WHEN acct_nbr = '3020' AND journal_code = 'CD'
    THEN amount ELSE 0.00 END),
COUNT(DISTINCT CASE WHEN acct_nbr = '3020' AND journal_code IN
('PJ', 'TJ')
              THEN source ELSE NULL END)
INTO j_tally, c_total, d_tally, e_total, f_total, k_tally
FROM GeneralLedger AS GL
WHERE period BETWEEN start_period AND end_period;
```

Exceptions:
Sometimes the UNION [ALL] is what you actually want. The other set operations in SQL-92, EXCEPT [ALL], and INTERSECT [ALL] are not widely available yet.

6.11 Testing SQL

When you are first writing a schema, you will probably generate some test data. If you look in the literature, there is a thing called an Armstrong set, which is the minimal number of rows that will test all of the constraints in a schema. Although it is difficult to automatically create an Armstrong set, you can do a good job with a little effort.

6.11.1 Test All Possible Combinations of NULLs

Rationale:
NULLs behave strangely, and if there are problems, there is a good chance that a NULL will be involved. Newbies using graphic tools often leave more NULL-able columns in a single table than a professional would in an entire schema for a Fortune 500 company payroll.

Exceptions:
If the number of combinations is excessive, then look at a redesign rather than a stress test. It means you probably have too many NULL-able columns in the schema.

6.11.2 Inspect and Test All CHECK() Constraints

Rationale:
You can extract the CHECK() constraint predicates from the DDL and look at them. The first thing is to see if the same data element has the same rules in all of the tables. Some attributes will always have the same CHECK() constraints if the model is correct. For example, the data type, regular expression, and check digit for a UPC code will be the same everywhere in the schema.

Some attributes may have different constraints in different tables. For example, it would be reasonable to have "quantity INTEGER DEFAULT 0 NOT NULL CHECK (quantity >= 0)" almost everywhere that the quantity attribute appears. However, you might find that there is also a "CHECK (quantity > 0)" on a table. Is this an error or a situation where a zero quantity is disallowed? You need to look and see.

Exceptions:
None

6.11.3 Beware of Character Columns

Rationale:
Character columns seldom have enough constraints on them. The result is that they have extra blanks in them, allow mixed-case letters, and will pretty much hold any kind of garbage that a user wishes to put in them.

My favorite piece of test data for oversized, unconstrained NVARCHAR(n) columns is a collection of Buddhist sutras in Chinese unicode. At least the users will learn a bit of classic Buddhist thought.

Exceptions:
None

6.11.4 Test for Size

Rationale:
One of the problems with small test data sets is that they will run just fine in the development shop, but when the size of the tables grows larger, you can get gradually degraded performance or catastrophe points. A catastrophe point is when there is a sudden change in the performance—the straw that breaks the camel's back. There is usually a physical component to a catastrophe point, such as excessive paging to a hard drive. Frankly, there is not a lot you can do about it except wait and see if it was a fluke or if it happens again.

Gradually degraded performance is the nicer of the two situations. You can monitor the system, see the loss, and take action before anything bad happens. The bad news is that the term *gradual* can be very short. The query that ran so well on a few thousand rows of test data is a pig when it goes live on several million rows of production data. Try to stress test on a data set that is larger than the current production database. That will let you know you have some margin of error.

Exceptions:
None

How to Use VIEWS

The Blind Men and the Elephant

By John Godfrey Saxe (1816–1887)

It was six men of Indostan
To learning much inclined,
Who went to see the Elephant
(Though all of them were blind),
That each by observation
Might satisfy his mind.

The First approached the Elephant,
And happening to fall
Against his broad and sturdy side,
At once began to bawl:
"God bless me! but the Elephant
Is very like a wall!"

The Second, feeling of the tusk,
Cried, "Ho! what have we here
So very round and smooth and sharp?
To me 'tis mighty clear
This wonder of an Elephant

Is very like a spear!"

The Third approached the animal,
And happening to take
The squirming trunk within his hands,
Thus boldly up and spake:
"I see," quoth he, "the Elephant
Is very like a snake!"

The Fourth reached out an eager hand,
And felt about the knee.
"What most this wondrous beast is like
Is mighty plain," quoth he;
"Tis clear enough the Elephant
Is very like a tree!"

The Fifth, who chanced to touch the ear,
Said: "E'en the blindest man
Can tell what this resembles most;
Deny the fact who can
This marvel of an Elephant
Is very like a fan!"

The Sixth no sooner had begun
About the beast to grope,
Than, seizing on the swinging tail
That fell within his scope,
"I see," quoth he, "the Elephant
Is very like a rope!"

And so these men of Indostan
Disputed loud and long,
Each in his own opinion
Exceeding stiff and strong,
Though each was partly in the right,
And all were in the wrong!

Moral:
So oft in theologic wars,
The disputants, I ween,
Rail on in utter ignorance

Of what each other mean,
And prate about an Elephant
Not one of them has seen!

VIEWs are virtual tables, defined by SELECT statements stored in the database. The SQL statement that defines the VIEW is executed only when the VIEW is invoked in another statement. The standard says that VIEWs are to act as if they are materialized, but in practice the optimizer will decide to materialize them as physical tables or to insert the SELECT statement in the definition into the query, invoking it and then compiling it like a derived table. There are six basic uses for VIEWs that we will discuss.

7.1 VIEW Naming Conventions Are the Same as Tables

Rationale:

A VIEW is a logical table. It consists of rows and columns, exactly the same as a base table. A VIEW can be used in SELECT, UPDATE, DELETE, and INSERT statements in the same way that a base table can. Therefore, it stands to reason that VIEWs should utilize the same naming conventions as are used for tables. As an aside, the same can be said for aliases, synonyms, derived tables, table-valued functions, or anything that returns a table.

In particular, there is an absurd naming convention of putting a "v" or "vw" in the first or last position of a VIEW name. My guess is that it comes from programmers either who are used to weakly typed languages that use Hungarian notation or who worked with file systems that had to have prefixes to locate the physical drive for the file. In the ISO-11179, the "vw" implies that the VIEW is a table dealing with Volkswagens.

Individuals who have a need to differentiate between tables and VIEWs can utilize the schema information tables to determine which objects are VIEWs and which objects are tables. They should be at the system administration level or higher.

INSERT, UPDATE, and DELETE are operations that cannot be performed on certain types of VIEWs. Users who need to do these privileges can be given INSTEAD OF triggers and never know if they are dealing with a VIEW or a base table.

Exceptions:

None

7.1.1 Always Specify Column Names

Rationale:

When creating VIEWs, SQL provides the option of specifying new column names for the VIEW clause or defaulting to the same column names as the defining SELECT statement. It is always advisable to explicitly specify VIEW column names instead of allowing them to default, even if using the same names as the underlying base tables. This will provide for more accurate documentation.

Exceptions:

Make sure that the VIEW clause names are correct. If you misspell them, that is what the user sees.

7.2 VIEWs Provide Row- and Column-Level Security

One of the most beneficial purposes served by VIEWs is to extend the data security features of SQL. VIEWs can be created that provide a subset of rows, a subset of columns, or a subset of both rows and columns from the base table.

How do VIEWs help provide row- and column-level security? Consider a "Personnel" table that contains all of the pertinent information regarding an enterprise's employees. Typically, name, address, position, birthdate, and salary information would be contained in such a table. However, not every user will require access to all of this information. Specifically, it may become necessary to shield the salary information from most users. You can accomplish this by creating a VIEW that does not contain the salary column and then granting most users the ability to access the VIEW, instead of the base table. The salary column will not be visible to users of the VIEW.

Or perhaps you need to implement security at the row level. Consider a table that contains project information. Typically, this would include project name, purpose, start date, and who is responsible for the project. Assume that the security requirements for projects within your organization deem that only the employee who is responsible for the project can access the project data. By storing the authorization ID of the responsible employee in the "projects" table, a VIEW can be created using the CURRENT_USER value.

```
CREATE VIEW MyProjects (..)
AS
SELECT ..
```

```
  FROM Projects
 WHERE authorized_user = CURRENT_USER;
```

Or, if you need to limit access to a team, you can create a table of teams to which only team managers have access.

```
CREATE VIEW MyProjects (..)
AS
SELECT ..
  FROM Projects AS P
 WHERE CURRENT_USER
       IN (SELECT team_user_id
             FROM ProjectTeams AS PT
            WHERE P.team_nbr = PT.team_nbr);
```

Another trick is to use the CURRENT_TIMESTAMP or CURRENT_DATE in VIEWs to get an automatic update to schedules and other time-related events.

```
CREATE TABLE AssignmentSchedule
(ssn CHAR(9) NOT NULL
     REFERENCES Personnel(ssn)
     ON UPDATE CASCADE
     ON DELETE CASCADE,
 task_code CHAR(5) NOT NULL,
 start_date TIMESTAMP NOT NULL,
 end_date TIMESTAMP NOT NULL,
 CHECK (start_date < end_date),
 PRIMARY KEY (upc, start_date));

CREATE VIEW Assignments (now, ssn, task_code)
AS
SELECT CURRENT_TIMESTAMP, ssn, task_code
  FROM AssignmentSchedule
 WHERE CURRENT_TIMESTAMP BETWEEN start_date AND end_date;
```

Each time the VIEW is invoked, it will check the clock and see if anything has changed for you.

7.3 VIEWs Ensure Efficient Access Paths

By coding the appropriate join criteria into the VIEW definition SQL, you can ensure that the correct join predicate will always be used. Of course, this technique becomes more useful as the SQL becomes more complex.

7.4 VIEWs Mask Complexity from the User

Somewhat akin to coding appropriate access into VIEWs, complex SQL can be coded into VIEWs to mask the complexity from the user. This can be extremely useful when your shop employs novice SQL users (whether those users are programmers, analysts, managers, or typical end users).

As an example, consider the code for a relational division. Relational division is one of the eight basic operations in Codd's (1979) relational algebra. The idea is that a divisor table is used to partition a dividend table and produce a quotient or results table. The quotient table consists of those values of one column for which a second column had all of the values in the divisor.

This is easier to explain with an example. We have a table of pilots and the planes they can fly (dividend); we have a table of planes in the hangar (divisor); we want the names of the pilots who can fly every plane (quotient) in the hangar. To get this result, we divide the PilotSkills table by the planes in the hangar.

```
CREATE TABLE PilotSkills
(pilot CHAR(15) NOT NULL,
 plane CHAR(15) NOT NULL,
 PRIMARY KEY (pilot, plane));

CREATE TABLE Hangar
 (plane CHAR(15) NOT NULL PRIMARY KEY);
```

Here is one way to write the query:

```
CREATE VIEW QualifiedPilots (pilot)
AS
SELECT DISTINCT pilot
  FROM PilotSkills AS PS1
 WHERE NOT EXISTS
       (SELECT *
          FROM Hangar
```

```
WHERE NOT EXISTS
      (SELECT *
         FROM PilotSkills AS PS2
        WHERE (PS1.pilot = PS2.pilot)
          AND (PS2.plane = Hangar.plane)));
```

This not the sort of thing that newbie SQL programmers can pull out of their hats, but they can write "SELECT pilot FROM QualifiedPilots;" without much trouble. Furthermore, the VIEW definition can be changed, and the user will never know it. Here is another version of relational division:

```
CREATE VIEW QualifiedPilots (pilot)
AS
SELECT PS1.pilot
  FROM PilotSkills AS PS1, Hangar AS H1
 WHERE PS1.plane = H1.plane
 GROUP BY PS1.pilot
HAVING COUNT(PS1.plane) = (SELECT COUNT(plane) FROM Hangar);
```

7.5 VIEWs Ensure Proper Data Derivation

Another valid usage of VIEWs is to ensure consistent derived data by creating new columns for VIEWs that are based on arithmetic formulae (e.g., creating a VIEW that contains a column named "tot_comp," which is defined by [salary + commission + bonus]). Because this column name is at the table level, it can be used in the SELECT of the invoking SELECT statement. That is, this is illegal:

```
SELECT emp_id, (salary + commission + bonus) AS tot_comp
  FROM Payroll
 WHERE tot_comp > 12000.00;
```

and this is legal:

```
CREATE VIEW PayrollSummary (emp_id, tot_comp)
AS
SELECT emp_id, (salary + commission + bonus)
  FROM PayrollSummary;
```

followed by:

```
SELECT emp_id, tot_comp
  FROM PayrollSummary
 WHERE tot_comp > 12000.00;
```

Although this is an easy formula, it is a good idea to have a complicated one in only one place in the schema. It might not be right, but at least it will be consistent.

7.6 VIEWs Rename Tables and/or Columns

You can rename columns in VIEWs. This is particularly useful if a table contains arcane or complicated column names. There are some prime examples of such tables in the schema information tables of most SQL products. Additionally, if other tables exist with clumsy table and/or column names, VIEWs can provide a quick solution until you can rename them. In many SQL products, doing this can require dropping and recreating the tables.

7.7 VIEWs Enforce Complicated Integrity Constraints

Consider a schema for a chain of stores that has three tables, thus:

```
CREATE TABLE Stores
(store_nbr INTEGER NOT NULL PRIMARY KEY,
 store_name CHAR(35) NOT NULL,
 ..);

CREATE TABLE Personnel
(ssn CHAR(9) NOT NULL PRIMARY KEY,
 last_name CHAR(15 NOT NULL,
 first_name CHAR(15 NOT NULL,
 ..);
```

The first two tables explain themselves. The third table shows the relationship between stores and personnel—namely, who is assigned to which job at which store and when this happened. Thus:

```
CREATE TABLE JobAssignments
(store_nbr INTEGER NOT NULL
```

```
        REFERENCES Stores (store_nbr)
        ON UPDATE CASCADE
        ON DELETE CASCADE,
ssn CHAR(9) NOT NULL PRIMARY KEY
        REFERENCES Personnel( ssn)
        ON UPDATE CASCADE
        ON DELETE CASCADE,
start_date TIMESTAMP DEFAULT CURRENT_TIMESTAMP NOT NULL,
end_date TIMESTAMP CHECK (start_date <= end_date),
job_type INTEGER DEFAULT 0 NOT NULL
          CHECK (job_type BETWEEN 0 AND 99),
PRIMARY KEY (store_nbr, ssn, start_date));
```

Let job_type 0 = "unassigned", 1 = "stockboy", and so on, until we get to 99 = "Store Manager"; we have a rule that each store has one and only one manager. In full SQL-92 you could write a constraint like this:

```
CHECK (NOT EXISTS
       (SELECT store_nbr
          FROM JobAssignments
         WHERE job_type = 99))
         GROUP BY store_nbr
        HAVING COUNT(*) > 1))
```

But many SQL products do not allow CHECK () constraints that apply to the table as a whole, and they do not support the scheme-level CREATE ASSERTION statement. So, how to do this? You might use a trigger, which will involve—ugh!—procedural code. Despite the SQL/PSM and other standards, most vendors implement different trigger models and use their proprietary 4GL language, but, being a fanatic, I want a pure SQL solution.

Let's create two tables like this:

```
CREATE TABLE Job_99_Assignments
(store_nbr INTEGER NOT NULL PRIMARY KEY
        REFERENCES Stores (store_nbr)
        ON UPDATE CASCADE
        ON DELETE CASCADE,
ssn CHAR(9) NOT NULL
        REFERENCES Personnel (ssn)
        ON UPDATE CASCADE
```

```
        ON DELETE CASCADE,
start_date TIMESTAMP DEFAULT CURRENT_TIMESTAMP NOT NULL,
end_date TIMESTAMP CHECK (start_date <= end_date),
job_type INTEGER DEFAULT 99 NOT NULL
        CHECK (job_type = 99));

CREATE TABLE Job_not99_Assignments
(store_nbr INTEGER NOT NULL
        REFERENCES Stores (store_nbr)
        ON UPDATE CASCADE
        ON DELETE CASCADE,
ssn CHAR(9) NOT NULL PRIMARY KEY
        REFERENCES Personnel (ssn)
        ON UPDATE CASCADE
        ON DELETE CASCADE,
start_date TIMESTAMP DEFAULT CURRENT_TIMESTAMP NOT NULL,
end_date TIMESTAMP CHECK (start_date <= end_date),
job_type INTEGER DEFAULT 0 NOT NULL
        CHECK (job_type BETWEEN 0 AND 98)—no 99 code
);
```

Then build a UNION-ed VIEW:

```
CREATE VIEW JobAssignments (store_nbr, ssn, start_date,
end_date, job_type)
AS
(SELECT store_nbr, ssn, start_date, end_date, job_type
   FROM Job_not99_Assignments
  UNION ALL
 SELECT store_nbr, ssn, start_date, end_date, job_type
   FROM Job_99_Assignments)
```

The key and job_type constraints in each table working together will guarantee only one manager per store. The next step is to add INSTEAD OF triggers to the VIEW, so that the users can insert, update, and delete from it easily.

As an exercise for the reader: How would you ensure that no store has more than two assistant managers?

7.8 Updatable VIEWs

The SQL-92 standard is actually conservative about which VIEWs are updatable. They have to be based on the following:

1. A SELECT statement on one and only one table, but the VIEW can be defined on several layers of VIEWs on top of VIEWs.
2. The VIEW must include all of the columns of a UNIQUE or PRIMARY KEY constraint in the base table. This guarantees that all of the rows in the VIEW map back to one and only one row in the base table from which it is derived.
3. All base table columns not shown in the VIEW must have default values or be NULL-able. The reason for that is obvious: You have to delete or insert a complete row into the base table, so the system must be able to construct such a row.

However, other VIEWs are updatable, and some vendors support more than the basic version given in the SQL-92 standard. The VIEW must have an INSERT, UPDATE, and DELETE rule under the covers, which maps its rows back to a single row in the base table(s).

7.8.1 WITH CHECK OPTION clause

Another feature, which is not used enough, is the WITH CHECK OPTION clause on a VIEW. It is a bit tricky, when you nest VIEWs inside each other, but the idea is that an UPDATE or INSERT INTO statement cannot leave the scope of the set selected by the updatable VIEW. For example, we have a VIEW like this:

```
CREATE VIEW NewYorkSalesmen (ssn, name, ..)
AS
SELECT ssn, name, ..
  FROM Salesmen
 WHERE city = 'New York';

And we update it, thus:

UPDATE NewYorkSalesmen
   SET city = 'Boston';
```

The result would be that "NewYorkSalesmen" would be empty when you come back to it. This is probably not desirable. However, if we had defined the updatable VIEW as:

```
CREATE VIEW NewYorkSalesmen (ssn, name, ..)
AS
SELECT ssn, name, ..
  FROM Salesmen
 WHERE city = 'New York'
WITH CHECK OPTION;
```

the system would test the update for a violation and would reject it.

7.8.2 INSTEAD OF Triggers

Because some VIEWs cannot be updated, you can add INSTEAD OF triggers to fool the users. This trigger is executed instead of the INSERT, UPDATE, or DELETE action, thus overriding the actions of the triggering statements. The syntax will vary from product to product, but expect something like this:

```
CREATE TRIGGER <trigger name>
ON <table name >
 [BEFORE | AFTER | INSTEAD OF]
 [INSERT| DELETE | UPDATE]
AS [<sql stmt> | BEGIN ATOMIC {<sql stmt>;} END]
```

For obvious reasons, only one INSTEAD OF trigger per INSERT, UPDATE, or DELETE statement can be defined on a table or VIEW. However, it is possible to define VIEWs on VIEWs where each VIEW has its own INSTEAD OF trigger. INSTEAD OF triggers are not allowed on updatable VIEWs that have a WITH CHECK OPTION.

You can also define INSTEAD OF triggers on base tables, but this is a bit weird because you have BEFORE and AFTER triggers.

7.9 Have a Reason for Each VIEW

Rationale:

VIEWs should be created only when they achieve a specific, reasonable goal. Each VIEW should have a specific application or business requirement that it fulfills before it is created. That requirement should be documented somewhere, preferably in a data dictionary or possibly as a remark in the VIEW declaration.

Exceptions:
None

7.10 Avoid VIEW Proliferation

Rationale:
The proliferation avoidance rule is based on common sense. Why create something that is not needed? It just takes up space that could be used for something that is needed.

Whenever a SQL object is created, additional entries are placed in the schema information tables. Creating needless schema objects causes what Craig Mullins calls *catalog clutter*. For example, in DB2, every unnecessary VIEW that is created in SQL will potentially insert rows into four VIEW-specific schema information tables (i.e., SYSVTREE, SYSVLTREE, SYSVIEWS, and SYSVIEWDEP) and three table-specific schema information tables (i.e., SYSTABLES, SYSTABAUTH, and SYSCOLUMNS).

It is a good idea to use a utility program to see if you have VIEWs that are not referenced anywhere. Another good idea is to see if you have VIEWs that do the same thing, or almost the same thing, so you can remove one of them.

Exceptions:
None

7.11 Synchronize VIEWs with Base Tables

Rationale:
Whenever a base table changes, all VIEWs that depend on that base table should be analyzed to determine if the change affects them. All VIEWs should remain logically pure. The VIEW should remain useful for the specific reason you created it.

For example, say a VIEW was created to control employee access to a project and we add the new badge numbers to the Personnel table. This badge number probably should also be added to the access VIEW. The badge number column can be added to the Personnel table immediately and then to the VIEW at the earliest convenience of the development team.

The synchronization rule requires that strict change impact analysis procedures be in place. Every change to a base table should trigger the usage of these utility programs and maintenance procedures.

Exceptions:
None

7.12 Improper Use of VIEWs

Over the years, VIEWs have been used for other purposes that made sense at the time but have been rendered obsolete with the advent of new DBMS functionality.

7.12.1 VIEWs for Domain Support

Rationale:
It is a sad fact of life that most RDBMS do not support domains. Domains were in the original relational model and should have been part of SQL from the start. A domain basically identifies the valid range of values that a column can contain. Of course, domains are more complex than this simple explanation. For example, only columns pooled from the same domain should be able to be compared within a predicate (unless explicitly overridden).

Some of the functionality of domains can be implemented using VIEWs and the WITH CHECK OPTION clause, which ensures the update integrity of VIEWs. This will guarantee that all data inserted or updated using the VIEW will adhere to the VIEW specification.

```
CREATE VIEW Personnel (ssn, name, sex,  ..)
AS
SELECT ssn, name, sex, ..
  FROM ISBN0008 — a name you did not want anyone to see
 WHERE sex IN (0, 1, 2) — iso codes
WITH CHECK OPTION;
```

Now, this method of using VIEWs to simulate domains is still viable, but a better technique to provide the same functionality is available—namely, CHECK() constraints.

```
CREATE TABLE Personnel
(ssn CHAR(9) NOT NULL, name, sex,  ..)
 ..
```

```
sex INTEGER DEFAULT 0 NOT NULL
    CHECK (sex IN (0, 1, 2)),
..);
```

And a CHECK() constraint is simpler than creating VIEWs with the WITH CHECK OPTION.

Exceptions:
None

7.12.2 Single-Solution VIEWs

Rationale:
Another past usage for VIEWs was to enable solutions where VIEWs really were the only way to solve a data access problem. Without VIEWs, some complex data access requests could be encountered that were not capable of being coded using SQL alone. However, sometimes a VIEW can be created to implement a portion of the access. Then, the VIEW can be queried to satisfy the remainder.

Consider the scenario where you want to report on detail information and summary information from a single table. For instance, what if you would like to report on stock prices? For each stock, provide all stock details, and also report the maximum, minimum, and average prices for that stock. Additionally, report the difference between the average price and each individual price.

```
CREATE VIEW StockSummary (ticker_sym, min_price, max_price,
avg_price)
AS
SELECT ticker_sym, MIN(price), MAX(price), AVG(price)
  FROM Portfolio
 GROUP BY ticker_sym;
```

After the VIEW is created, the following SELECT statement can be issued joining the VIEW to the base table, thereby providing both detail and aggregate information on each report row:

```
SELECT P.ticker_sym, P.quote_date, S.min_price, S.max_price,
S.avg_price,
       (P.price - S.avg_price) AS fluctuation
  FROM Portfolio AS P, StockSummary AS S
 WHERE P.ticker_sym = S.ticker_sym;
```

Situations such as these were ideal for using VIEWs to make data access a much simpler proposition. However, the advent of table expressions (sometimes referred to as in-line VIEWs) makes this usage of VIEWs obsolete. Why? Instead of coding the VIEW, we can take the SQL from the VIEW and specify it directly into the SQL statement that would have called the VIEW. Using the previous example, the final SQL statement becomes:

```
SELECT P.ticker_sym, S.min_price, S.max_price, S.avg_price,
       (P.price - S.avg_price) AS fluctuation
  FROM Portfolio AS P,
       (SELECT ticker_sym, MIN(price), MAX(price), AVG(price)
          FROM Portfolio
         GROUP BY ticker_sym) AS S
 WHERE P.ticker_sym = S.ticker_sym;
```

So we can use a table expression to avoid creating and maintaining a VIEW.

Exceptions:
If an expression is used in many places and it has a clear meaning in the data model, then create a VIEW.

7.12.3 Do Not Create One VIEW Per Base Table

Rationale:
A dubious recommendation is often made to create one VIEW for each base table in a SQL application system. This is what Craig Mullins calls "The Big VIEW Myth." This is supposed to insulate application programs from database changes. This insulation is to be achieved by mandating that all programs be written to access VIEWs instead of base tables. When a change is made to the base table, the programs do not need to be modified because they access a VIEW, not the base table.

There is no adequate rationale for enforcing a strict rule of one VIEW per base table for SQL application systems. In fact, the evidence supports not using VIEWs in this manner. Although this sounds like a good idea in principle, indiscriminate VIEW creation should be avoided. The implementation of database changes requires scrupulous analysis regardless of whether VIEWs or base tables are used by your applications. Consider the simplest kind of schema change, adding a column to a table. If you do not add the column to the VIEW, no programs can access that column unless another VIEW is created that contains that column. But if you create a new VIEW every time you add a new column, it will not take long for your environment to be swamped with VIEWs.

Then you have to ask which VIEW should be used by which program? Similar arguments can be made for removing columns, renaming tables and columns, combining tables, and splitting tables.

In general, if you follow good SQL/SQL programming practices, you will usually not encounter situations where the usage of VIEWs initially would have helped program/data isolation anyway. By dispelling, "The Big VIEW Myth," you will decrease the administrative burden of creating and maintaining an avalanche of base table VIEWs.

Exceptions:
None

7.13 Learn about Materialized VIEWs

Rationale:
A materialized VIEW is brought into existence in the physical database, where it can be used like any other table. This is implementation dependent, so you have to know what your product does to get the best use of this feature.

All VIEWs are supposed to act as if they are materialized, but in practice the text of the view can often be put into the parse tree of the statement using it and expanded like an in-line macro statement. For example, given this VIEW:

```
CREATE VIEW NewYorkSalemen (ssn, first_name, ..)
AS
SELECT ssn, first_name, ..
  FROM Personnel
 WHERE city = 'New York';
```

When it is used in a query, the effect is as if it were a derived table expression inside that query. For example:

```
SELECT ssn, first_name, ..
  FROM NewYorkSalemen
WHERE firstname = 'Joe';
```

in effect becomes:

```
SELECT ssn, first_name, ..
  FROM (SELECT ssn, first_name, ..
          FROM Personnel
         WHERE city = 'New York')
       AS NewYorkSalemen (ssn, first_name, ..)
 WHERE firstname = 'Joe';
```

which will probably become something like this in the parse tree:

```
SELECT ssn, first_name, ..
  FROM Personnel AS NewYorkSalemen (ssn, first_name, ..)
 WHERE city = 'New York'
   AND firstname = 'Joe';
```

However, if more than one user references a VIEW, it can be cheaper to materialize it once and share the data among all users. If the materialized result set is small enough to fit into main storage, the performance improvements are even greater.

This is actually a common event, because we tend to build views that summarize data for reporting periods. Thus, lots of users want to get to the same summary views at the same time. If you plan the VIEWs to take advantage of this usage pattern, you can get major performance improvements.

Exceptions:
None

How to Write Stored Procedures

"Whatever language you write in, your task as a programmer is to do the best you can with the tools at hand. A good programmer can overcome a poor language or a clumsy operating system, but even a great programming environment will not rescue a bad programmer."

—Kernighan and Pike

EVERY SQL PRODUCT has some kind of 4GL tools that allow you to write stored procedures that reside in the database and that can be invoked from a host program. Each 4GL is a bit different, but they are all block-structured languages. They have varying degrees of power and different language models. For example, T-SQL is a simple, one-pass compiler modeled after the C and Algol languages. It was not intended as an application development language, but rather as a tool for doing short tasks inside a SQL Server database.

At the other extreme, Oracle's PL/SQL is modeled after ADA and SQL/PSM. It is a complicated language that can be used for application development. Likewise, Informix 4GL is an application development language that generates C code, which can be immediately ported to a large number of platforms.

What this means is that anything I say about SQL stored procedures will have to be general, but perhaps the most frightening thing is that I have to go back and teach basic software engineering

principles to SQL programmers. If you look at the SQL code posted in newsgroups, much of it is written as if all of the work done in the 1970s and 1980s by Yourdon, DeMarco, Dijkstra, Wirth, and others. never happened. Wake up, people! Those rules still apply to any programming language because they apply to programming.

8.1 Most SQL 4GLs Are Not for Applications

Rationale:

Most of the proprietary procedural languages added to SQL by vendors were never meant to replace application development languages (note the exceptions). They were meant to be micro-languages that could be used for procedural operations inside the database.

The classic micro-language has no real input/output (I/O); you can print a message on the standard system output and that is about all. There is no file control, no complex computations, and no display formatting functions. These languages were for writing triggers and short cleanup modules in the schema, and the rule of thumb was never to have a procedure over one page or 50 lines long.

This is fine; in a tiered architecture, display and complex computations are done in the host language of the presentation layer. But if you read the SQL newsgroups, you will constantly find newbie programmers who want to do display formatting in the database. They want to add leading zeros in a SELECT statement, concatenate first and last names, put line numbers on the result set to display ranges of those line numbers, and a host of other things. SQL is strictly a data-retrieval language and has nothing to do with application presentation layers.

Exceptions:

Informix 4GL, Progress, Oracle's PL/SQL, and a few other languages were actually meant for application development. Sometimes the language came before the SQL database and vice versa. A proprietary language can be fast to execute, fast to write, and have lots of nice features. A lot of mainframe packages are implemented in Informix 4GL under the covers, Oracle sells packages written in PL/SQL, and a lot of midsized systems are implemented in Progress. The trade-off is the ability to maintain these proprietary code bases versus maintaining a standard programming language with embedded SQL.

8.2 Basic Software Engineering

I am amazed that so many SQL programmers do not know basic software engineering. Working programmers on newsgroups actually have to ask for definitions of cohesion and coupling. Apparently, programmers are not getting the basics of their trade and simply try to pass certification exams instead of actually learning their craft. With some embarrassment, I will now give what should have been covered in a freshman course.

These principles apply to any procedural programming language, but they have slightly different applications in SQL because it is a nonprocedural, set-oriented language with concurrency issues.

8.2.1 Cohesion

Cohesion is how well a module does one and only one thing: that it is logically coherent. The modules should have strong cohesion. You ought to name the module in the format "<verb><object>," where the "<object>" is a specific logical unit in the data model.

There are several types of cohesion. They are ranked here from the worst form of cohesion to the best:

1. Coincidental
2. Logical
3. Temporal
4. Procedural
5. Communicational
6. Informational
7. Functional

This scale is an ordinal scale, and a module can have characteristics of more than one type of cohesion in it. Let's define terms as follows:

- *Coincidental cohesion*. This is the worst kind of cohesion. This is where a module performs several unrelated tasks under one roof. Think of someone pasting random blocks of code together and somehow getting it to compile. This is what you get with dynamic SQL or passing table names as parameters.

For example, "InsertNewCustomer()" tells you that you are going to be working with the tables related to the customers. However, a procedure called "InsertNewRecord," which can put a row into any table in the schema, is too general to have good cohesion. It works on bagpipes, marriages, and octopi or any new table that gets put into the schema later.

Programmers should not be using dynamic SQL, because it has no cohesion and is dangerous. Users who have to provide, say, a table name, can also provide extra SQL code that will be executed. For example, instead of passing just the table name, they pass "Foobar; DELETE FROM Foobar; COMMIT" and destroy the database. But dynamic SQL also says that the programmer is so incompetent that he or she could not write the program and had to give the job to any random user, present or future, to complete on the fly.

This kind of coding is the result of trying to do metadata operations in an application by using the schema information tables. SQL engines have tools for metadata, and the user should not be writing versions of them.

- *Logical cohesion*. Here modules can perform a series of related tasks, but the calling module selects only one. The worst example of this was a posting in 2004 on a SQL Server newsgroup where a programmer had been ordered to put all procedures into one module. A parameter would then pick which of 50-plus modules would be executed and which parameters would be used and what they would do in context.

  OO programmers like to do this for each table, because they can think of each table as some kind of object, and the procedure looks like methods on that object. It isn't.

- *Temporal cohesion*. The module performs a series of actions that are related in time. The classic example is to put all startup or shutdown actions in one module. Older COBOL and file system programmers tend to do this because they worked with batch processing systems that did not have concurrency issues.

- *Procedural cohesion*. The modules perform a sequence of steps in a process that has to be executed in specific order. Again, this style is used by file system programmers who are used to batch processing systems. They often write a lot of temporary tables to hold the process steps, like we used to allocate working tapes.

- *Communicational cohesion*. All elements operate on the same input data set or produce the same output data set. The parts communicate via common data in a global table.
- *Informational cohesion*. This is also called *sequential cohesion* in the literature. Output from one element in the module serves as input for some other element, but unlike logical cohesion, the code for each action is completely independent.
- *Functional cohesion*. The module performs exactly one function or achieves a single goal. Math functions are the best example of this kind of cohesion. This is what we are trying to do, and it is why SQL is also known as a functional language.

Procedural, communicational, informational, and functional cohesion are a bit more complicated in SQL than in 3GL programming because we have transactions. A transaction is logically one step, although it consists of individual SQL statements. What looks like procedural, communicational, or informational cohesion can be much stronger in SQL.

8.2.2 Coupling

If modules have to be used in a certain order, then they are strongly coupled. If they can be executed independently of each other and put together like Lego blocks, then they are loosely or weakly coupled. There are several kinds of coupling, which are ranked from worst to best as follows:

1. Content
2. Common
3. Control
4. Stamp
5. Data

The types of coupling are defined as follows:

- *Content coupling*. This occurs when one module directly references the contents of another module. For example, module *x* branches to a local label in module *y* or module *x* modifies a statement of module *y*. Such modules are inextricably linked to each other.

Content coupling is dangerous but is not often supported in SQL 4GL products. The rule here is not to pass a procedure as a parameter in a SQL 4GL.

- *Common coupling*. This occurs when several modules have access to the same global data. In the 3GL languages, this was use of global variables in the C family and other languages. In SQL, this can happen with the use of common global tables to pass information. It gets to be dangerous when concurrency controls are not done right.
- *Control coupling*. This occurs when one module has control over the logic of another. If module *x* calls module *y* and *y* determines which action *x* must take, then control coupling is present. The passing of a control switch statement as an argument is an example of control coupling. In SQL, you do this with subqueries that reference other parts of the schema in predicates that drive control flow.
- *Stamp coupling*. Entire tables are passed to the called module, but only some columns are used. In SQL, the use of "SELECT *" in production code is the prime example.
- *Data coupling*. Two modules are data coupled if all arguments are scalar data elements. Data coupling is a desirable goal because such modules are easier to maintain. Any changes in one module or table are less likely to cause a regression fault in the others.

8.3 Use Classic Structured Programming

Although I like to say that SQL is short for "Scarcely Qualifies as a Language," the truth is that it came from "Structured English-like Query Language" from the original project at IBM. A lot of current programmers seem to have missed the structured revolution and have reverted back to ad hoc programming but call it "extreme" or "agile" these days to make sloppy programming sound better.

In classic structured programming, you have three control structures:

1. *Concatenation*. The statements inside brackets are executed in sequential order. In SQL/PSM this is shown with the keyword brackets "BEGIN [ATOMIC] .. END" and often by just "BEGIN.. END" in proprietary 4GLs. The keyword ATOMIC makes the block into a transaction, which we will not discuss in detail here.

2. *Selection*. A Boolean expression determines which one of two blocks of statements is executed. In SQL/PSM this is shown with the keywords "IF .. THEN .. [ELSE ..] END IF;" and in proprietary 4GLs with "IF .. THEN .. [ELSE ..];" or "IF .. [ELSE ..];" but syntax is always enough alike not to be a problem.
3. *Iteration*. A block of statements is repeatedly executed while a Boolean expression is TRUE. In SQL/PSM this is shown with the keywords "WHILE .. LOOP.. END WHILE;" and you will see "WHILE.. DO.." keywords in many products. Again, various products are always enough alike not to be a problem.

The important characteristic of all of these control structures is that they have one entry and one exit point. Any code written using them will also have one entry and one exit point. You do not use a GO TO statement in classic structured programming.

Some languages allowed a RETURN() statement to jump out of functions and set the value of the function call. Some allowed a switch or case expression as a multiway selection control statement. But by sticking as close as possible to classic structured programming, your code is safe, verifiable, and easy to maintain.

8.3.1 Cyclomatic Complexity

So is there a heuristic for telling if I have a bad stored procedure? There are a lot of metrics actually. In the 1970s, we did a lot of research on software metrics and came up with some good stuff. Here is one that can be computed by hand when you have short procedures to measure.

Tom McCabe (1976) invented the cyclomatic complexity metric. The score is basically the number of decision points in a module plus one, or the number of execution paths through the code. Decision points are where a flow graph of the procedure would branch. In a well-structured 4GL program, the keywords of the language will tell us what the decision points are. For us that means IF, WHILE, and each branch of a CASE or SWITCH statement, if your 4GL supports that feature.

If the module has a score of 1 to 5, it is a simple procedure. If the score is between 6 to 10, it might need simplification. If the score is greater than 10, then you really should simplify the module. There are other metrics and methods, but most of them are not as easy to compute on the fly.

8.4 Avoid Portability Problems

Rationale:

We already talked about writing portable SQL statements, but you also need to write portable 4GL code. Because these languages are proprietary, they will have some features that will not port to other SQL 4GLs. Also, you cannot expect that you will always find programmers who are expert in these languages or who have time to become experts. Plain, simple code in an unfamiliar language can be a great help.

Stick to the classic three control structures. They will always port with only mechanical syntax changes and can be read by any programmer who knows a typical 3GL language. But there are other tricks and heuristics.

8.4.1 Avoid Creating Temporary Tables

In some vendor languages, the programmer can create a temporary table on-the-fly, while in Standard SQL the temporary tables are only created by someone holding administrative privileges. Use subquery expressions, derived tables, or VIEWs instead. The use of temporary tables is usually a sign of a bad design. Temporary tables are most often used to hold the steps in a procedural process. They replace the scratch or work tapes we used in the 1950s magnetic tape file systems.

There are two major types of error handling. The Sybase/SQL Server family uses a sequential code model. After executing each statement, the SQL engine sets a global error variable, and the programmer has to write code to immediately catch this value and take action.

The SQL/PSM model uses an interrupt model. There is a global SQLSTATE (the old SQLCODE is deprecated), which can return multiple values into a cache. These values can trigger actions that were defined in WHENEVER statements associated with blocks of code. Maintaining the error handling part of a module is difficult, so do a lot of comments in it.

Put as much of the code into SQL statements, not into the 4GL. Ideally, a stored procedure ought to be one SQL statement, perhaps with a few parameters. The next best design would be a "BEGIN [ATOMIC] .. END" with a straight sequence of SQL statements. You lose points for each "IF..THEN..ELSE" and lose lots of points for each loop.

8.4.2 Avoid Using Cursors

Rationale:
A cursor is a way of converting a set into a sequential file so that a host language can use it. There are a lot of options on the Standard SQL cursor, and there are a lot of vendor options, too.

Cursors are difficult to port and generally run much slower than pure nonprocedural SQL statements. By slower, I mean orders of magnitude slower. For safety, the SQL engine has to assume that anything can happen inside a cursor, so it puts the transaction at the highest level it can and locks out other users.

So why do people use them? The overwhelming reason is ignorance of SQL and old habits. The cursors in SQL are modeled after tape file semantics, and people know that kind of procedural programming. Here is the analogy in detail:

```
ALLOCATE <cursor name> = get a tape drive on a channel
DECLARE <cursor name> CURSOR FOR .. = mount a tape and have a
record declaration for the file.
OPEN <cursor name> = open the file.
FETCH <cursor orientation> <cursor name> INTO <local variables>
= read one record at a time in the program then move the read/
write head as oriented.
CLOSE <cursor name> = close the file
DEALLOCATE <cursor name> = free tape drive
```

Add the use of temporary tables as working or scratch tapes and you can mimic a 1950s tape system statement for statement and never learn to think relationally at all. In 2004, there was an example of this in the SQL Server Programming newsgroup. The newbie had written one cursor to loop through the first table and select rows that met a criterion into a temporary table. A second cursor looped through a second table ordered on a key; inside this loop, a third cursor looped through the temporary table to match rows and do an update. This was a classic 1950s master/transaction tape file merge but written in SQL. The 25 or so statements used in it were replaced by one UPDATE with a scalar subquery expression. It ran almost three orders of magnitude faster.

Exceptions:
The only uses I have found are truly exceptional. Cursors can be used to repair poorly designed tables that have duplicate rows or data that is so trashed you have to look at every row by itself to clean the data before

doing an ALTER TABLE to fix such poor design permanently. Here are some reasons to use cursors:

1. Cursors can be used to build metadata tools, but you really should be using what the vendor has provided. Messing directly with schema information tables is dangerous.

2. Cursors can be used to solve NP-complete problems in SQL where you stop with the first answer you find that is within acceptable limits. The "Traveling Salesman" and "Bin Packing" problems are examples, but they are not exactly common database problems and are better solved with a procedural language and backtracking algorithms.

3. In T-SQL and other products that still use physically contiguous storage, calculating a median is probably much faster with a cursor than with any of the set-based solutions, but in other products with different storage or indexing, computing the median is trivial.

4. It is possible to actually write code that is worse than a cursor. Consider this slightly cleaned-up posting by Curtis Justus in the SQL Server Programming newsgroup in November 2004. He had a table of approximately 1 million rows and needed to "do something with each of the rows" in what he called a traditional "For/Each" type algorithm. The specifications were never explained beyond that. He posted a pseudocode program in T-SQL dialect, which would translate into Standard SQL pseudocode something like this:

```
CREATE PROCEDURE TapeFileRoutine()
BEGIN
-- assume temporary table as a sequential scratch tape
DECLARE maxrecs INTEGER;
DECLARE current_row INTEGER;
DECLARE temp_a INTEGER;
DECLARE temp_b INTEGER;

INSERT INTO ScratchTape (record_nbr, temp_a, temp_b)
SELECT {{proprietary_auto_increment}}, col1, col2
  FROM MyBigTable;
```

```
SET maxrecs = (SELECT COUNT(*) FROM ScratchTape);
SET current_row = 0;

WHILE (current_row < maxrecs)
DO
-- Get the values
SELECT col_1, col_2
  INTO temp_a, temp_b
  FROM ScratchTape
 WHERE rec_id = current_row;
-- do my manipulation ;
SET current_row = current_row + 1;
END WHILE;
END;
```

Yes, you are looking at a sequential tape file algorithm from the 1950s written in SQL in the early 21st century. The poster wanted to know if this was the most efficient way to go after the data. The answer, obviously, is that even a cursor would be better than this approach.

You would be surprised by how many newbies rediscover sequential tape processing in SQL. Perhaps even more remarkable was this person's attitude that he was currently getting a fast enough response time that it did not have to be coded correctly. The lack of portability, the orders of magnitude degradation, and the extra lines of code that had to be maintained were simply not regarded as his responsibility as a professional.

8.4.3 Prefer Set-Oriented Constructs to Procedural Code

Rationale:

The optimizer cannot use control structures from the 4GL to pick an execution plan. Thus, the more logic you can pass to it via pure SQL statements, the better it will perform. The real cost in a stored procedure is in data access. Timing for various operations on a typical 1-GHz PC in summer 2001 in nanoseconds was:

```
Execute single instruction = 1 ns (1/1,000,000,000) sec
Fetch word from L1 cache memory = 2 ns
Fetch word from main memory = 10 ns
Fetch word from consecutive disk location = 200 ns
Fetch word from new disk location (seek) = 8,000,000 ns
```

If I can save a few disk fetches, I get a much better return on my efforts than if I write faster executing computations. The seek times have not gotten and are not going to get much better in the foreseeable future.

8.4.3.1 Use CASE Expressions to Replace IF-THEN-ELSE Control Flow Statements

As an example of how to do this, consider the problem of updating the prices in a bookstore. This is a version of an exercise in an early Sybase SQL training class to show why we needed cursors. We want to take 10 percent off expensive books ($25 or more) and increase inexpensive books by 10 percent to make up the loss. The following statement is the first impulse of most new SQL programmers, but it does not work.

```
CREATE PROCEDURE IncreasePrices()
LANGUAGE SQL
DETERMINISTIC
BEGIN
UPDATE Books
   SET price = price * 0.90
 WHERE price >= 25.00;
UPDATE Books
   SET price = price * 1.10
 WHERE price < 25.00;
END;
```

A book priced at $25.00 is reduced to $22.50 by the first update. Then it is raised to $24.75 by the second update. Reversing the order of the update statements does not change the problem. The answer given in the course was to use a cursor and to update each book one at a time. This would look something like this:

```
BEGIN
DECLARE BookCursor CURSOR
FOR SELECT price FROM Books
FOR UPDATE;
 ..
ALLOCATE BookCursor;
 ..
OPEN BookCursor;
FETCH Bookcursor;
WHILE FOUND
```

```
DO
IF price >= 25.00
THEN
UPDATE Books
   SET price = price * 0.90
 WHERE CURRENT OF BookCursor;
ELSE
UPDATE Books
   SET price = price * 1.10
 WHERE CURRENT OF BookCursor;
END IF;
FETCH NEXT Bookcursor;
END WHILE;
 ..
CLOSE BookCursor;
DEALLOCATE BookCursor;
END;
```

But by using a CASE expression to replace the IF..THEN..ELSE logic, you can write:

```
UPDATE Books
   SET price = CASE WHEN price >= 25.00
               THEN price * 0.90;
               ELSE price * 1.10 END;
```

This requires less code and will run faster. The heuristic is to look for nearly identical SQL statements in the branches of an IF statement, then replace them inside one statement with a CASE expression.

8.4.3.2 Use Sequence Tables to Replace Loop Control Flow

A sequence table is a single-column table that contains integers from 1 to (*n*), for some values of (*n*) that are large enough to be useful. One way of generating such a table is:

```
CREATE TABLE Sequence (seq INTEGER NOT NULL PRIMARY KEY);

CREATE PROCEDURE MakeSequence()
LANGUAGE SQL
DETERMINISTIC
BEGIN
```

```
INSERT INTO Sequence (seq) VALUES(1);
WHILE (SELECT MAX(seq) FROM Sequence) > 1000
DO INSERT INTO Sequence (seq)
   SELECT MAX(seq)+1 FROM Sequence;
END WHILE;
END;
```

However, it is faster to write:

```
CREATE TABLE Sequence (seq INTEGER NOT NULL PRIMARY KEY);

CREATE PROCEDURE MakeSequence()
LANGUAGE SQL
DETERMINISTIC
INSERT INTO Sequence (seq)
SELECT hundred * 100 + ten * 10 + unit + 1
  FROM (VALUES (0, 1, 2, 3, 4, 5, 6, 7, 8, 9)) AS Units(unit)
        CROSS JOIN
       (VALUES (0, 1, 2, 3, 4, 5, 6, 7, 8, 9)) AS Tens(ten)
        CROSS JOIN
       (VALUES (0, 1, 2, 3, 4, 5, 6, 7, 8, 9)) AS
Hundreds(hundred);
```

This use of CROSS JOINs is another example of how to avoid loops. A weird but useful heuristic is to put the phrase "the set of.." in front of the nouns in a sentence that describes the problem you are solving. It is bad grammar, but it can help shift your mindset to thinking in terms of sets.

Converting a string with a comma-separated list of values into a proper table with the position and value is done by using a simple WHILE loop that cuts off one substring up to but not including the comma, and then converts the substring to an integer. The code would look like this:

```
CREATE PROCEDURE Parser(IN input_string VARCHAR(255))
DETERMINISTIC
LANGUAGE SQL
BEGIN
DECLARE parm_nbr INTEGER; SET parm_nbr = 0;
DECLARE val INTEGER; SET val = CAST(NULL AS INTEGER);
SET input_string = TRIM (BOTH input_string);
```

```
WHILE CHAR_LENGTH(input_string) > 0
DO BEGIN
   SET parm_nbr = parm_nbr +1
   IF POSITION(','IN input_string) > 0
   THEN BEGIN
        SET val = SUBSTRING (input_string
                        FROM 1
                         FOR POSITION(',' IN input_string)-1);
        SET input_string = SUBSTRING (input_string
                                      FROM
CHAR_LENGTH(input_string)
                                            - POSITION(',' IN
input_string));
        END
   ELSE BEGIN
        SET val = input_string;
        SET input_string = '';—empty string
        END;
   IF END;
   INSERT INTO ParmList VALUES (parm_nbr, CAST(val AS INTEGER));
END WHILE;
END;
```

However, the same thing can be done with a Sequence table, thus:

```
CREATE PROCEDURE Parser(IN input_string VARCHAR(255))
DETERMINISTIC
LANGUAGE SQL
BEGIN
INSERT INTO ParmList (parm_nbr, parm)
SELECT COUNT(S2.seq),
       CAST (SUBSTRING (',' || input_string || ',' FROM
MAX(S1.seq + 1) FOR
                           (S2.seq - MAX(S1.seq + 1)))
         AS INTEGER)
  FROM Input_strings AS I1, Sequence AS S1, Sequence AS S2
 WHERE SUBSTRING (',' || input_string || ',' FROM S1.seq FOR 1)
= ','
   AND SUBSTRING (',' || input_string || ',' FROM  S2.seq FOR 1)
= ','
   AND S1.seq < S2.seq
   AND S2.seq <= CHAR_LENGTH (input_string) + 2
```

```
 GROUP BY input_string, S2.seq;
END;
```

It makes life easier if the lists in the input strings start and end with a comma. You will also need a table called Sequence, which is a set of integers from 1 to (*n*).

The S1 and S2 copies of Sequence are used to locate bracketing pairs of commas, and the entire set of substrings located between them is extracted and cast as integers in one nonprocedural step. The trick is to be sure that the left-hand comma of the bracketing pair is the closest one to the second comma. The place column tells you the relative position of the value in the input string. The real advantage of the nonprocedural approach comes from modifying this second procedure to handle an entire table whose rows are CSV strings.

```
CREATE TABLE InputStrings
(list_name CHAR(10) NOT NULL PRIMARY KEY,
 input_string VARCHAR(255) NOT NULL);

INSERT INTO InputStrings VALUES ('first', '12,34,567,896');
INSERT INTO InputStrings VALUES ('second', '312,534,997,896');
 ...
```

In fact, the one row at a time procedure can be replaced with a VIEW instead:

```
CREATE VIEW Breakdown (list_name, parm_nbr, param)
AS
SELECT list_name, COUNT(S2.seq),
      CAST (SUBSTRING (',' || I1.input_string || ',', MAX(S1.seq
+ 1),
                          (S2.seq - MAX(S1.seq + 1)))
         AS INTEGER)
  FROM InputStrings AS I1, Sequence AS S1, Sequence AS S2
 WHERE SUBSTRING (',' || I1.input_string || ',' FROM S1.seq FOR
1) = ','
   AND SUBSTRING (',' || I1.input_string || ',' FROM S2.seq FOR
1) = ','
   AND S1.seq < S2.seq
   AND S2.seq <= CHAR_LENGTH (I1.input_string) + 2
 GROUP BY I1.list_name, I1.input_string, S2.seq;
```

8.4.3.3 Use Calendar Tables to Perform Temporal Calculations

Rationale:

The first thing to do when you start a new application is to build a Sequence and Calendar table. The calendar table is keyed on a date, and the nonkey columns contain information about that date relative to the enterprise. Is this a workday or a holiday? What is its Julian date number? What fiscal calendar does it fall in? In short, anything to do with how the enterprise uses time must be detailed.

The table for 20 years of data is only about 7,050 rows, which is nothing. You can look up programming tricks with this table in newsgroups or in Celko (1999).

Exceptions:

None

8.4.3.4 Consider Auxiliary Tables to Perform Computations

Rationale:

If a function or computation returns only a few thousand values, instead of computing it over and over, put the parameters and the results into an auxiliary table that can be joined to the tables to get the answer. SQL is good at JOINs but not at computations; play to its strength.

Exceptions:

If the computation can be done with simple four-function math, then auxiliary tables could be overkill. If the computation is unpredictable or known to have a huge range, then it might not be possible to put it into an auxiliary table.

8.5 Scalar versus Structured Parameters

There are no arrays, lists, or other data structures in Standard SQL-92. There is only one data structure: the table. There are base tables, views, and derived tables, but the operative word in that list is "table."

Procedural languages depend on other data structures, such as arrays, lists, and records. Newbie programmers who learned to program with such structures want to use them desperately when they get to SQL. The result is that they kludge code with poor performance. Even worse, they use dynamic SQL to construct a statement or an entire program on the fly.

Stored procedure calls expect scalar parameters, not structured or dynamic parameters. By using a few coding tricks, you can still get the

advantages of stored procedures and have some flexibility. A typical problem is to pass a list of values to an IN() predicate, like this in pseudocode:

```
SELECT a, b, c FROM Foobar WHERE a IN (<<parameter list>>);
```

The all-too-common kludge is dynamic SQL, which has a string with a list of comma-separated values for <<parameter list>>. One answer is to use the code in section 8.4 to put the list into a table and write a compiled statement, thus:

```
SELECT a, b, c FROM Foobar WHERE a IN (SELECT aa FROM ParmList);
```

But a better answer is to scrub the list data in the front end and load it into a table with an INSERT INTO statement. The ability to do this will vary with each SQL product, but the standard SQL syntax uses row constructors, like this:

```
INSERT INTO Parmlist (parm) VALUES (1), (2), (3), (4);
```

The VALUES() list has to be of a known number of rows, but by putting NULLs or other dummy values in the list, you can get the effect of a dynamic list. You only need to clean them out on the database side, and you can use SELECT DISTINCT to remove duplicate values if needed. The full table insertion statement would look like this in the host language:

```
INSERT INTO Parmlist (parm)
SELECT DISTINCT parm
  FROM (VALUES (:h1), (:h2), (:h3), (:h4)) AS X(parm)
 WHERE X.parm IS NOT NULL;
```

8.6 Avoid Dynamic SQL

Dynamic SQL is both slow and dangerous. It is also a sign that the programmer did not have a proper design for his or her application and is now turning that job over to any user, present or future. The purpose of Dynamic SQL is to build metadata tools, not applications. A metadata tool treats schema objects as schema objects, not as parts of a data model.

8.6.1 Performance

A stored procedure will have a cached execution plan in most SQL products, but Dynamic SQL has to be prepared repeatedly with each execution. Obviously, this is going to be slower than running compiled code that might already be in main storage. One counterargument is that if the predicates change in some significant way, then recompiling can give a better execution plan. The gist of this execution model is that if I have a predicate with constants instead of parameters, the optimizer can do a better job with it. For example, given this simple query:

```
SELECT name, rank, serial_nbr
  FROM CombatMarines
 WHERE sex = :input_sex_code;
```

If the parameter ":input_sex_code" is male (1, using the ISO sex codes), then a table scan is the best way to process the query; if the parameter is female (2, using the ISO sex codes), then an index is the best; if the parameter is anything else, simply return an empty result set.

Obviously, this is implementation dependent. However, more modern optimizers will create several possible execution plans, based on the statistics, and hold them until the parameter is known. In short, we are back to the "Trust the optimizer" rule.

8.6.2 SQL Injection

SQL injection is a security attack in which the attacker places SQL code into your procedure and executes it. Whenever you let a user input code directly into Dynamic SQL in stored procedure or SQL statements generated in client code, you are in danger. Here is an example of a function that builds a simple Dynamic SQL string, based on an FAQ at esquel@sommarskog.se:

```
CREATE FUNCTION Search_Orders (custname VARCHAR(60))
RETURNS VARCHAR(3000)
RETURN ('SELECT * FROM Orders WHERE '
        || COALESCE (custname, '1=1'));
```

Assume that the input for the parameters "custname" comes directly from user input without any filtering or validation and that a malicious user passes this value in:

```
SET custname = ' 1=1; DROP TABLE Orders;';

The resulting SQL statement becomes:

'SELECT * FROM Orders WHERE 1=1; DROP TABLE orders;'
```

The host program can then PREPARE and EXECUTE it, and drop the table for you.

A plain user is not likely to have permissions to drop a table, but I can run all kinds of statements I wish via SQL injection. The attacker looks for inputs that will produce a syntax error rather than a runtime error, so he or she knows there is Dynamic SQL on the database side. The attacker writes the code, and, if needed, ends it with semicolons or with a start of comment that will remove the rest of the query code from compilation. With a little probing, the attacker can find out if the Dynamic SQL is providing a table name and really trash the schema.

The first defense is not to give the users more privileges than are necessary for their jobs. A good heuristic is that plain users should be granted only SELECT privileges on the tables with which they work, but the best defense is not to use Dynamic SQL in production code.

Heuristics

THE FOLLOWING TRICKS and heuristics are not exactly mathematically precise scientific methods. In fact, some of them sound pretty weird, but as Larry Constantine once remarked, a method is a list of things that tells you what to do next, when you did not know what to do next, and you hope the method at least gets you to a workable solution, if not a good solution.

Let me pick simple programming problems and apply these heuristics as we go along. Consider the "Dance Partner Problem" in which you are given a list of people and their gender. Your task is to pair them into couples.

```
CREATE TABLE People
(name VARCHAR (35) NOT NULL PRIMARY KEY,
 gender INTEGER DEFAULT 1 NOT NULL
 CHECK (gender IN (1,2)); —iso gender codes
```

Then there is the classic Orders problem: Given a data model of orders from customers for products from inventory, answer any of several questions. This is not a complete schema, but it will work for demonstration purposes.

```
CREATE TABLE Orders
(order_nbr INTEGER NOT NULL,
 ..);

CREATE TABLE OrdersDetails
(order_nbr INTEGER NOT NULL
        REFERENCES Orders (order_nbr)
        ON UPDATE CASCADE
        ON DELETE CASCADE,
 sku  CHAR(10) NOT NULL
       REFERENCES Inventory (sku)
       ON UPDATE CASCADE
       ON DELETE CASCADE,
 description CHAR(20) NOT NULL,
 qty INTEGER NOT NULL CHECK(qty > 0),
 unit_price DECIMAL(12,4) NOT NULL,
 ..);
```

9.1 Put the Specification into a Clear Statement

This might sound obvious, but the operative word is *clear* statement. You need to ask questions at the start. Let me give some examples from actual problem statements having to do with a schema that models a typical orders and order details database:

1. *"I want to see the most expensive item in each order."* How do I handle ties for the most expensive item? Did you mean the highest unit price or the highest extension (quantity × unit price) on each order?
2. *"I want to see how many lawn gnomes everyone ordered."* How do I represent someone who never ordered a lawn gnome in the result set? Is that a NULL or a zero? If they returned all of their lawn gnomes, do I show the original order or the net results? Or do I show no order ever as a NULL and returns as a zero to preserve information?
3. *"How many orders were over $100?"* Did you mean strictly greater than $100 or greater than or equal to $100?

In the "Dance Partner" example, we need to ask:

1. How do we pair the couples?
2. What do we do if there are more boys than girls (or vice versa) in the table?
3. Can someone have more than one partner? If so, how do we assign them?

Writing specs is actually harder than writing code. Given a complete, clear specification, the code can almost write itself.

9.2 Add the Words "Set of All..." in Front of the Nouns

The big leap in SQL programming is thinking in sets and not in process steps that handle one unit of data at a time. Phrases like "for each x..." poison your mental model of the problem. Look for set characteristics and not for individual characteristics. For example, given the task to find all of the orders that ordered exactly the same number of each item, how would you solve it?

One approach is, for each order, to see if there are two values of quantity that are not equal to each other and then reject that order. This leads to either cursors or a self-join. Here is a self-join version; I will not do the cursor version.

```
SELECT D1.order_nbr
  FROM OrderDetails AS D1
 WHERE NOT EXISTS
       (SELECT *
          FROM OrderDetails AS D2
         WHERE D1.order_nbr = D2.order_nbr
           AND D1.qty <> D2.qty);
```

Or you can look at each order as a set with these set properties:

```
SELECT order_nbr
  FROM OrderDetails
 GROUP BY order_nbr
HAVING MIN(qty) = MAX(qty);
```

9.3 Remove Active Verbs from the Problem Statement

Words like *traverse, compute,* or other verbs that imply a process will poison your mental model. Try to phrase it as a "state of being" description instead. This is the same idea as in section 9.2, but with a slight twist.

Programmers coming from procedural languages think in terms of actions. They add numbers, whereas a declarative programmer looks at a total. They think of process, whereas we think of completed results.

9.4 You Can Still Use Stubs

A famous Sydney Harris cartoon shows the phrase "Then a miracle occurs" in the middle of a blackboard full of equations, and a scientist says to the writer, "I think you should be more explicit here in step 2."

We used that same trick in procedural programming languages by putting in a stub module when we did not know what to do at the point in a program. For example, if you were writing a payroll program and the company had a complex bonus policy that you did not understand or have specifications for, you would write a stub procedure that always returned a constant value and perhaps sent out a message that it had just executed. This allowed you to continue with the parts of the procedure that you did understand.

This is more difficult to do in a declarative language. Procedural language modules can be loosely coupled, whereas the clauses and subqueries of a SELECT statement are a single unit of code. You could set up a "test harness" for procedural language modules; this is more difficult in SQL.

Looking at the "Dance Partner Problem," I might approach it by saying that I need the boys and the girls in two separate subsets, but I don't know how to write the code for that yet. So I stub it with some pseudocode in my text editor. Because this is for dance, let's pick the pseudocode words from a musical. Nobody is going to see this scratch paper work, so why not?

```
SELECT M1.name AS male, F1.name AS female
  FROM (<miracle for guys>) AS M1(name, <join thingie for guys>)
       FULL OUTER JOIN
       (<miracle for dolls>) AS F1(name, <join thingie for
dolls>)
       ON M1.<join thingie for guys> ?? F1.<join thingie for
dolls>;
```

The angle-bracketed pseudocode might expand to multiple columns, subqueries, or just about anything later. Right now they are placemarkers. I also have a "??" placemarker for the relationship between my guys and dolls. I can then go to the next level in the nesting and expand the (<miracle for guys>) subquery like this:

```
(SELECT P1.name, <join thingie for guys>
   FROM People AS P1
  WHERE P1.gender = 1)
 AS M1 (name, <join thingie for guys>)
```

The same pattern would hold for the (<miracle for dolls>) subquery. I now need to figure out some way of getting code for <join thingie for guys>. The first place I look is the columns that appear in the People table. The only thing I can find in that table is gender. I have a rule that tells me guys = 1 and dolls = 2, and I am enforcing it in my subqueries already. (Note: The full ISO sex codes are 0 = unknown, 1 = male, 2 = female, and 9 = lawful persons, corporations, etc.) I could try this:

```
SELECT M1.name AS male, F1.name AS female
  FROM (SELECT P1.name, P1.gender
          FROM People AS P1
          WHERE P1.gender = 1) AS M1 (name, gender)
       FULL OUTER JOIN
       (SELECT P1.name, gender
          FROM People AS P1
         WHERE P1.gender = 2) AS F1 (name, gender)
       ON M1.gender = 1
          AND F1.gender = 2;
```

but it is pretty easy to see that this is a CROSS JOIN in thin disguise. Add something with the names, perhaps?

```
SELECT M1.name AS male, F1.name AS female
  FROM (SELECT P1.name, P1.gender
          FROM People AS P1
          WHERE P1.gender = 1) AS M1 (name, gender)
       FULL OUTER JOIN
       (SELECT P1.name, gender
          FROM People AS P1
         WHERE P1.gender = 2) AS F1 (name, gender)
```

```
ON M1.gender = 1
   AND F1.gender = 2
   AND M1.name <= F1.name;
```

There was no help there. It produces a smaller set of pairs, but you still get multiple couples on the dance floor. This is where some experience with SQL helps. One of the customary programming tricks is to use a self-join to get a ranking of elements in a set based on their collation sequence. Because this works with any table, we can use it in both guys and dolls to get the final query.

```
SELECT M1.name AS male, F1.name AS female
  FROM (SELECT P1.name, COUNT (P2.name)
          FROM People AS P1, People AS P2
          WHERE P2.name <= P1.name
            AND P1.gender = 1
            AND P2.gender = 1
          GROUP BY P1.name) AS M1 (name, rank)
       FULL OUTER JOIN
       (SELECT P1.name, COUNT (P2.name)
          FROM People AS P1, People AS P2
         WHERE P2.name <= P1.name
           AND P1.gender = 2
           AND P2.gender = 2
         GROUP BY P1.name) AS F1 (name, rank)
       ON M1.rank = F1.rank;
```

9.5 Do Not Worry about Displaying the Data

In a tiered architecture, display is the job of the front end, not the database. Obviously, you do not do rounding, add leading zeros, change case, or pick a date format in the database. The important thing is to pass the front end all of the data it needs to do its job, but it is more than that. You can get your dance partner pairs with the query in section 9.4, but if you do not want to see the pairs on the same row, you can write a more compact query like this:

```
SELECT P1.name, P1.gender, COUNT(P2.name) AS rank
  FROM People AS P1, People AS P2.
  WHERE P1.gender = P2.gender
    AND P2.name <= P1.name
```

```
GROUP BY P1.name, P1.gender;
```

This will put one person per row with a ranking in the alphabetical sort for their gender rather than one couple per row, but that is still the same information from a simpler query. Notice that both solutions can leave unpaired people toward the end of the alphabet.

You can add an ORDER BY clause to the cursor that passes the result set to the front-end program in a simple client/server system, but in architectures with multiple tiers, sorting and other display functions might be performed differently in several places. For example, the same data is displayed in English units sorted by division in the United States but displayed in SI units sorted by country in Europe.

9.6 Your First Attempts Need Special Handling

Henry Ledgard (1976) put it very nicely:

> Pruning and restoring a blighted tree is almost an impossible task. The same is true of blighted computer programs. Restoring a structure that has been distorted by patches and deletions, or fixing a program with a seriously weak algorithm isn't worth the time. The best that can result is a long, inefficient, unintelligible program that defies maintenance. The worst that could result, we dare not think of.

This is especially true with SQL, but how to handle restarts in DDL and DML is different because of the declarative nature of the two sublanguages. DDL execution is static once it is put into place, whereas DML is dynamic. That is, if I issue the same CREATE <schema object> command, it will have the same results each time, but if I issue the same SELECT, INSERT, UPDATE, or DELETE, the execution plan could change each time.

9.6.1 Do Not Be Afraid to Throw Away Your First Attempts at DDL

Bad DDL will distort all of the code based on it. Just consider our little "Dance Partner" schema: What if a proprietary BIT data type had been used for gender? The code would not port to other SQL dialects. The host languages would have to handle low-level bit manipulation. It would not interface with other data sources that use ISO standards.

Designing a schema is hard work. It is unlikely that you will get it completely right in one afternoon. Rebuilding a database will take time and require fixing existing data, but the other choices are worse.

When I lived in Salt Lake City, Utah, a programmer I met at a user group meeting had gotten into this situation: The existing database was falling apart as the workload increased thanks to poor design at the start. The updates and insertions for a day's work were taking almost 24 hours at that time, and the approaching disaster was obvious to the programmers. Management had no real solution, except to yell at the programmers. They used the database to send medical laboratory results to hospitals and doctors.

A few months later, I got to see how an improperly declared column resulted in the wrong quantities of medical supplies being shipped to an African disaster area. The programmer tried to save a little space by violating first normal form by putting the package sizes into one column and pulling them out with SUBSTRING() operations. The suppliers later agreed to package smaller quantities to help with the fantastic expense of shipping to a war zone. Now the first "subfield" in the quantity column was one unit and not five, but the tightly coupled front did not know this. Would you like to pick which four children will die because of sloppy programming? See what we mean by the last sentence in Ledgard's quote?

9.6.2 Save Your First Attempts at DML

Bad DML can run several orders of magnitude slower than good DML. The bad news is that it is difficult to tell what is good and what is bad in SQL. The procedural programmers had a deterministic environment in which the same program ran the same way every time. SQL decides how to execute a query based on statistics about the data and the resources available. They can and do change over time. Thus, what was the best solution today could be the poorer solution tomorrow.

In 1988, Pascal (1988) published a classic article on PC database systems at the time. Pascal constructed seven logical equivalent queries for a database. Both the database and the query set were simple and were run on the same hardware platform to get timings.

The Ingres optimizer was smart enough to find the equivalence, used the same execution plan, and gave the best performance for all queries. The other products at the time gave uneven performances. The worst timing was an order of magnitude or more than the best. In the case of Oracle, the worst timing was more than 600 times the best.

I recommend that you save your working attempts so that you can reuse them when the world and/or your optimizer change. The second example for the "Dance Partner" in section 9.5 does a nice job of illustrating this heuristic. Put the code for one of the queries in as a comment, so the maintenance programmer can find it.

9.7 Do Not Think with Boxes and Arrows

This is going to sound absolutely insane, but some of us like to doodle when we are trying to solve a problem. Even an informal diagram can be a great conceptual help, especially when you are learning something new. We are visual creatures.

The procedural programmers had the original ANSI X3.5 Flowchart symbols as an aid to their programming. This standard was a first crude attempt at a visual tool that became Structure Charts and Data Flow Diagrams (DFD) in the 1970s. All of these tools are based on "boxes and arrows"—they show the flow of data and/or control in a procedural system. If you use the old tools, you will tend to build the old systems. You might write the code in SQL, but the design will tend toward the procedural.

9.8 Draw Circles and Set Diagrams

If you use set-oriented diagrams, you will tend to produce set-oriented solutions. For example, draw a GROUP BY as small, disjointed circles inside a larger containing circle so you see them as subsets of a set. Use a time line to model temporal queries. In a set-oriented model, nothing flows; it exists in a state defined by constraints.

Probably the clearest example of "boxes and arrows" versus "set diagrams" is the Adjacency List model versus the Nested Sets model for trees. You can Google these models or buy a copy of my book *Trees and Hierarchies in SQL for Smarties* for details. The diagrams for each approach are shown in Figure 9.1.

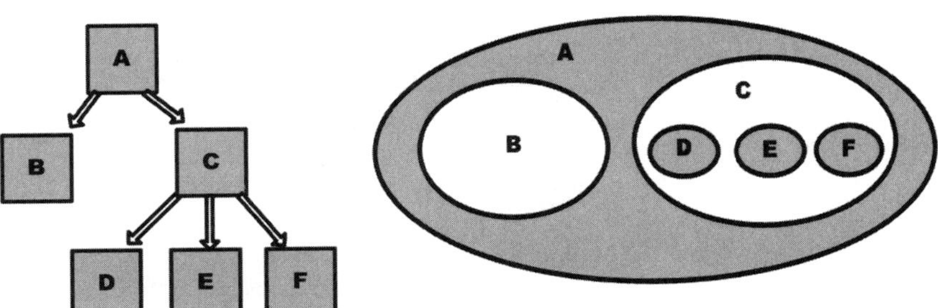

Figure 9.1 *Adjacency list versus Nested Set Trees.*

9.9 Learn Your Dialect

Although you should always try to write Standard SQL, it is also important to know which constructs your particular dialect and release favor. For example, constructing indexes and keys is important in older products that are based on sequential file structures. At the other extreme, the Nucleus engine from Sand Technology represents the entire database as a set of compressed bit vectors and has no indexing because in effect everything is automatically indexed.

9.10 Imagine That Your WHERE Clause Is "Super Ameba"

That is the weirdest title in this chapter, so bear with me. Your "Super Ameba" computer can split off a new processor at will, and assign it a task, in a massively parallel fashion. Imagine that every row in the working table that was built in the FROM clause is allocated one of these "ameba processors" that will test the WHERE clause search condition on just that row. This is a version of Pournelle's rule: "one task, one processor."

If every row in your table can be independently tested against simple, basic search conditions, then your schema is probably a good relational design. But if your row needs to reference other rows in the same table, consult an outside source, or cannot answer those simple questions, then you probably have some kind of normalization problems.

You have already seen the Nested Sets model and the Adjacency List model for trees. Given one row in isolation from the rest of the table, can you answer a basic node question about the tree being modeled? This leads to asking: What are basic questions? Here is a short list that applies to trees in graph theory.

1. Is this a leaf node?
2. Is this the root node?
3. How big is the subtree rooted at this node?
4. Given a second node in the same tree, is this node superior, subordinate, or at the same level as my node?

Question 4 is particularly important, because it is the basic comparison operation for hierarchies. As you can see, the Nested Sets model can answer all of these questions and more, whereas the Adjacency List model can answer none of them.

9.11 Use the Newsgroups and Internet

The Internet is the greatest resource in the world, so learn to use it. You can find a whole range of newsgroups devoted to your particular product or to more general topics. When you ask a question on a newsgroup, please post DDL, so that people do not have to guess what the keys, constraints, Declarative Referential Integrity, data types, and so forth in your schema are. Sample data is also a good idea, along with clear specifications that explain the results you wanted.

Most SQL products have a tool that will spit out DDL in one keystroke. Unfortunately, the output of these tools is generally less than human-readable. You should prune the real tables down to just what is needed to demonstrate your problem: There is no sense in posting a 100-column CREATE TABLE statement when all you want is two columns. Then clean up the constraints and other things in the output using the rules given in this book. You are asking people to do your job for you for free. At least be polite enough to provide them with sufficient information.

If you are a student asking people to do your homework for you, please be advised that presenting the work of other people as your own is a valid reason for expulsion and/or failure at a university. When you post, announce that this is homework, the name of your school, your class, and your professor. This will let people verify that your actions are allowed.

Thinking in SQL

"It ain't so much the things we don't know that get us into trouble. It's the thing we know that just ain't so."
—Artemus Ward (Charles Farrar Browne), American humorist (1834–1867)

THE BIGGEST HURDLE in learning SQL is thinking in sets and logic, instead of in sequences and processes. I just gave you a list of heuristics in the previous chapter, but let's take a little time to analyze why mistakes were made. You now have some theory, but can you do diagnostics?

I tried to find common errors that new programmers make, but perhaps the most difficult thing to learn is thinking in sets. Consider the classic puzzle shown in Figure 10.1.

The usual mistake people make is trying to count the 1 × 1 × 2 bricks one at a time. This requires the ability to make a three-dimensional mental model of the boxes, which is really difficult for most of us.

The right approach is to look at the whole block as if it were completely filled in. It is 4 × 5 × 5 units, or 50 bricks. The corner that is knocked off is 3 bricks, which we can count individually, so we must have 47 bricks in the block. The arrangement inside the block does not matter at all.

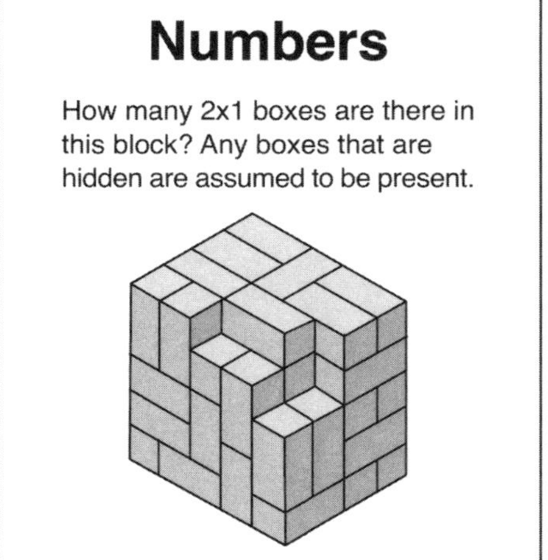

Numbers
How many 2x1 boxes are there in this block? Any boxes that are hidden are assumed to be present.

Figure 10.1 *Classic block puzzle.*

All of these examples are based on actual postings in a newsgroup that have been translated into SQL/PSM to remove proprietary features. In some cases, I have cleaned up the data element names, and in others I have left them. Obviously, I am guessing at motivation for each example, but I think I can defend my reasoning.

10.1 Bad Programming in SQL and Procedural Languages

As an example of not learning any relational approaches to a problem, consider a posting in the comp.databases.ms-sqlserver newsgroup in January 2005: The title was "How to Find a Hole in Records," which already tells you that the poster is thinking in terms of a file system and not an RDBMS.

The original table declaration had the usual newbie "id" column, without a key or any constraints. The table modeled a year's worth of rows identified by a week-within-year number (1 to 53) and a day-of-the-week number (1 to 7). Thus, we started with a table that looked more or less like this, after the names were cleaned up:

```
CREATE TABLE WeeklyReport
(id INTEGER AUTONUMBER NOT NULL,—not valid SQL!
 week_nbr INTEGER NOT NULL,
 day_nbr INTEGER NOT NULL);
```

By removing the useless, proprietary id column and adding constraints, we then had the following table:

```
CREATE TABLE WeeklyReport
(week_nbr INTEGER NOT NULL
          CHECK(week_nbr BETWEEN 1 AND 53),
 day_nbr INTEGER NOT NULL
         CHECK(day_nbr BETWEEN 1 AND 7),
PRIMARY KEY(week_nbr, day_nbr));
```

Despite giving some constraints in the narrative specification, the poster never bothered to apply them to the table declaration. Newbies think of a table as a file, not as a set. The only criteria that data needs to be put into a file is that it is written to that file. The file cannot validate anything. The proprietary auto-number acts to replace a nonrelational record number in a sequential file system.

The problem was to find the earliest missing day within each week for inserting a new row. If there were some other value or measurement for that date being recorded, it was not in the specifications. The poster's own T-SQL solution translated in SQL/PSM like this, with some name changes:

```
CREATE FUNCTION InsertNewWeekDay (IN my_week_nbr_nbr INTEGER)
RETURNS INTEGER
LANGUAGE SQL
BEGIN DECLARE my_day_nbr INTEGER;
DECLARE result_day_nbr INTEGER;
SET my_day_nbr = 1;
xx:
WHILE my_day_nbr < 8
DO IF NOT EXISTS
  (SELECT *
      FROM WeeklyReport
     WHERE day_nbr = my_day_nbr
       AND week_nbr = my_week_nbr_nbr)
THEN BEGIN
     SET result_day_nbr = my_day_nbr;
     LEAVE xx;
     END;
ELSE BEGIN
     SET my_day_nbr = my_day_nbr + 1;
```

```
     ITERATE xx;
     END;
END IF;
END WHILE;
RETURN result_day_nbr;
END;
```

This is a classic imitation of a FOR loop, or counting loop, used in all 3GL programming languages. However, if you look at it for two seconds, you will see that this is bad procedural programming! SQL will not make up for a lack of programming skills. In fact, the bad effects of mimicking 3GL languages in SQL are magnified. The optimizers and compilers in SQL engines are not designed to look for procedural code optimizations. By removing the redundant local variables and getting rid of the hidden GOTO statements in favor of a simple, classic structured design, the poster should have written this:

```
CREATE FUNCTION InsertNewWeekDay (IN my_week_nbr INTEGER)
RETURNS INTEGER
LANGUAGE SQL
BEGIN
DECLARE answer_nbr INTEGER;
SET answer_nbr = 1;
WHILE answer_nbr < 8
DO IF NOT EXISTS
     (SELECT *
         FROM WeeklyReport
        WHERE day_number = answer_nbr
          AND week_nbr = my_week_nbr)
   THEN RETURN answer_nbr;
   ELSE SET answer_nbr = answer_nbr + 1;
   END IF;
END WHILE;
RETURN CAST (NULL AS INTEGER);—cause an error
END;
```

This points out another weakness in this posting. We were not told how to handle a week that has all seven days represented. In the original table design, any integer value would have been accepted because of the lack of constraints. In the revised DDL, any weekday value not between 1 and 7 will cause a primary-key violation. This is not the best solution, but it at least follows the specs that were given without making too many guesses as to what should have been done.

But can we do this without a loop and get a pure, nonprocedural SQL solution? Yes, there are several ways: Because the purpose of finding this weekday number is to insert a row in the table, why not do that in one procedure instead of finding the number in a function, and then doing the insertion in another procedural step. Think at the level of a whole process and not in sequential steps.

This first answer is ugly looking and difficult to generalize, but it is fast if the optimizer factors out the tabular subquery in the WHEN clauses and computes it once. It also uses no local variables.

```
CREATE PROCEDURE InsertNewWeekDay (IN new_week_nbr INTEGER)
LANGUAGE SQL
INSERT INTO WeeklyReport (week_nbr, day_nbr)
VALUES (new_week_nbr,
      (CASE WHEN 1 NOT IN
           (SELECT day_nbr FROM WeeklyReport WHERE week_nbr =
new_week_nbr)
             THEN 1
             WHEN 2 NOT IN
            (SELECT day_nbr FROM WeeklyReport WHERE week_nbr =
new_week_nbr)
             THEN 2
             WHEN 3 NOT IN
            (SELECT day_nbr FROM WeeklyReport WHERE week_nbr =
new_week_nbr)
             THEN 3
             WHEN 4 NOT IN
            (SELECT day_nbr FROM WeeklyReport WHERE week_nbr =
new_week_nbr)
             THEN 4
             WHEN 5 NOT IN
            (SELECT day_nbr FROM WeeklyReport WHERE week_nbr =
new_week_nbr)
             THEN 5
             WHEN 6 NOT IN
            (SELECT day_nbr FROM WeeklyReport WHERE week_nbr =
new_week_nbr)
             THEN 6
             WHEN 7 NOT IN
```

```
            (SELECT day_nbr FROM WeeklyReport WHERE week_nbr =
new_week_nbr)
             THEN 7
             ELSE NULL END;—null will violate primary key
```

The thought process was to get the entire set of weekday numbers present in the week, and then compare them to each value in an ordered list. The CASE expression is just a way to hide that list. Although it is a step forward, it is not yet really a set-oriented solution.

Here is another version that uses a table constructor. This is more compact and easy to generalize. Here we are actually using a set-oriented solution! We are subtracting the set of actual days from the set of all possible days, and then looking at the minimum value in the result to get an answer.

```
CREATE PROCEDURE InsertNewWeekDay (IN new_week_nbr INTEGER)
LANGUAGE SQL
INSERT INTO WeeklyReport (week_nbr, day_nbr)
(SELECT my_week_nbr, MIN(n)
   FROM (VALUES (1), (2), (3), (4), (5), (6), (7)) AS Weekdays(n)
  WHERE NOT EXISTS
        (SELECT *
           FROM WeeklyReport AS W
          WHERE W.week_nbr = my_week_nbr
            AND Weekdays.n = W.my_day_nbr));
```

You can also use a pure set operations approach. The set difference operator can remove all of the numbers that are present, so that we can pick the minimum value from the leftovers.

```
CREATE PROCEDURE InsertNewWeekDay (IN new_week_nbr INTEGER)
LANGUAGE SQL
INSERT INTO WeeklyReport (week_nbr, day_nbr)
SELECT my_week_nbr, MIN(n)
FROM (VALUES (1), (2), (3), (4), (5), (6), (7)
      EXCEPT
      SELECT day_nbr
        FROM WeeklyReport AS W
       WHERE W.week_nbr = my_week_nbr) AS N(n);
```

If all seven days are present, we will get an empty set, which will return a NULL for the day_nbr, and the NULL will violate the primary-key constraint.

Here is a third, generalized version with the Sequence table providing any range of integers desired. Just remember that the DDL has to also match that change.

```
CREATE PROCEDURE InsertNewWeekDay (IN new_week_nbr INTEGER)
LANGUAGE SQL
INSERT INTO WeeklyReport (week_nbr, day_nbr)
SELECT my_week_nbr, MIN(n)
   FROM (SELECT seq FROM Sequence WHERE seq <= 7—change to any
value
         EXCEPT
         SELECT day_nbr
           FROM WeeklyReport AS W
          WHERE W.week_nbr = my_week_nbr) AS N(n);
```

In the case of only seven values, there is not going to be a huge difference in performance among any of these answers. However, with a huge number of values, the use of hashing or bit vector indexes would be a noticeable improvement over a loop.

10.2 Thinking of Columns as Fields

The original code was actually much worse, because the poster wanted to create and drop tables on the fly. The purpose is to load totals into a summary report table.

```
CREATE PROCEDURE SurveySummary()
LANGUAGE SQL
BEGIN
DECLARE sche_yes INTEGER;
DECLARE sche_no INTEGER;
DECLARE sche_mb INTEGER;
DECLARE sche_other INTEGER;

DECLARE how_yes INTEGER;
DECLARE how_no INTEGER;
DECLARE how_mb INTEGER;
DECLARE how_other INTEGER;
```

```
DECLARE paaexpl_yes INTEGER;
DECLARE paaexpl_no INTEGER;
DECLARE paaexpl_mb INTEGER;
DECLARE paaexpl_other INTEGER;

SET sche_yes = (SELECT COUNT(*) FROM SurveyForms WHERE sche =
1);
SET sche_no = (SELECT COUNT(*) FROM SurveyForms WHERE sche = 2);
SET sche_mb = (SELECT COUNT (*) FROM SurveyForms WHERE sche = 3);
SET sche_other = (SELECT COUNT(*)
                    FROM SurveyForms
                   WHERE NOT (sche IN (1, 2, 3)));

SET how_yes = (SELECT COUNT(*) FROM SurveyForms WHERE howwarr =
1);
SET how_no = (SELECT COUNT(*) FROM SurveyForms WHERE howwarr =
2);
SET how_mb = (SELECT COUNT (*) FROM SurveyForms WHERE howwarr =
3);
SET how_other = (SELECT COUNT(*)
                   FROM SurveyForms
                  WHERE NOT (howwarr IN (1,2,3)));

SET paaexpl_yes = (SELECT COUNT(*) FROM SurveyForms WHERE
paaexpl = 1);
SET paaexpl_no = (SELECT COUNT(*) FROM SurveyForms WHERE
paaexpl = 2);
SET paaexpl_mb = (SELECT COUNT (*) FROM SurveyForms WHERE
paaexpl
 = 3);
SET paaexpl_other = (SELECT COUNT(*) FROM SurveyForms WHERE NOT
(paaexpl IN (1, 2, 3)));

DELETE FROM SurveyWorkingtable;
INSERT INTO SurveyWorkingtable
VALUES (sche_yes, sche_no, sche_mb, sche_other,
        How_yes, how_no, how_mb, how_other,
        Paaexpl_yes, paaexpl_no, paaexpl_mb, paaexpl_other);
END;
```

Why did the poster create a dozen local variables and then use scalar subqueries to load them? The poster is still thinking in terms of a 3GL programming language. In COBOL or other 3GL languages, the file containing the Construction Survey data would be read in one record at a time, and then each record would be read one field at a time, from left to right. A sequence of IF-THEN statements would look at the fields and increment the appropriate counter. When the entire file is read, the results would be written to the working file for the survey summary.

The poster looked at each column as if it were a field and asked how to get the value for it, in isolation from the whole. The poster had seen the use of a subquery expression and implemented it that way. The subqueries will not be well optimized, so this is actually going to run longer than if the poster had used SQL/PSM to mimic the classic COBOL program for this kind of summary.

Without repeating a dozen columns again, a set-oriented solution is this:

```
CREATE PROCEDURE SurveySummary()
LANGUAGE SQL
BEGIN
DELETE FROM SurveyWorkingtable;
INSERT INTO SurveyWorkingtable (sche_yes, sche_no, ..,
paaexpl_other)
SELECT SUM (CASE WHEN sche = 1 THEN 1 ELSE 0 END) AS sche_yes,
       SUM (CASE WHEN sche = 2 THEN 1 ELSE 0 END) AS sche_no,
      ..
       SUM (CASE WHEN paaexpl NOT IN (1, 2, 3)
                 THEN 1 ELSE 0 END) AS paaexpl_other
 FROM SurveyForms;
END;
```

The trick was to ask what you want in each row of a summary table, as a completed unit of work, and not start at the column level. The answer is a tally of answers to some questions. The word *tally* leads you to SUM() or COUNT(), and you remember the trick with the CASE expression.

The final question is why not use a VIEW to get the summary instead of a procedure?

10.3 Thinking in Processes, Not Declarations

This is a simple schema for checking items out of an inventory. The original schema lacked keys and constraints that had to be added to give us this:

```
CREATE TABLE Users
(user_id CHAR(8) NOT NULL PRIMARY KEY,
 password VARCHAR(10) NOT NULL,
 max_reserves INTEGER NOT NULL
 CHECK (max_reserves >= 0));

CREATE TABLE Reservations
(user_id CHAR(8) NOT NULL
     REFERENCES Users(user_id)
     ON UPDATE CASCADE
     ON DELETE CASCADE,
item_id INTEGER NOT NULL
     REFERENCES Items(item_id));
```

The original narrative specification was:

> Each user can reserve a maximum of (*n*) items. Whenever a user reserves something, the "max_reserves" field [sic] of the user is retrieved and checked. Then a record [sic] is inserted into the Reservations table, and the "max_reserves" field [sic] of the user is updated accordingly. I would like to ask if there is a better way to implement this system, because there is a chance that the user reserves more than the maximum number, if he or she is logged in from two computers.

The first proposal was for a stored procedure that looked like this in SQL/PSM:

```
CREATE PROCEDURE InsertReservations (IN max_reserves INTEGER,
IN my_user_id CHAR(8), IN my_item_id INTEGER)
LANGUAGE SQL
BEGIN
DECLARE my_count INTEGER;
SET my_count
    = (SELECT COUNT(*)
         FROM Reservations
        WHERE user_id = my_user_id);
IF my_count >= max_reserves
THEN RETURN ('You have Reached you MAX number of items');
ELSE INSERT INTO Reservations (user_id, item_id)
     VALUES(my_user_id, my_item_id);
END IF;
END;
```

Passing the maximum number of items as a parameter makes no sense, because you have to look it up; this will let you pass any value you desire. Having a local variable for the count is redundant; SQL is orthogonal, and the scalar subquery can be used wherever the scalar variable is used.

Rows are not records and columns are not fields. SQL is a declarative language, not a procedural one. So a sequence of procedural steps like "Retrieve → check → insert → update" does not make sense. Instead, you say that you make a reservation such that the user is not over his or her limit. Think of logic, not process.

```
CREATE PROCEDURE MakeReservation
  (IN my_user_id CHAR(8), IN my_item_id INTEGER)
LANGUAGE SQL
BEGIN
INSERT INTO Reservations (user_id, item_id)
SELECT my_user_id, my_item_id
  FROM Users AS U
 WHERE U.user_id = my_user_id
    AND U.max_reserves
        >= (SELECT COUNT(*)
              FROM Reservations AS R
             WHERE R.user_id = my_user_id);
-- add error handling here
END;
```

Instead of recording the tally of reserved items in local storage, you can get it with a subquery expression. In fact, you might want to have a view to use for reports.

```
CREATE VIEW Loans (user_id, max_reserves, current_loans)
AS
SELECT U.user_id, U.max_reserves, COUNT(*)
  FROM Reservations AS R, Users AS U
 WHERE R.user_id = U.user_id
 GROUP BY U.user_id, U.max_reserves;
```

10.4 Thinking the Schema Should Look Like the Input Forms

There are several versions of this error. The easiest one is a simple timecard form that gets modeled exactly as it is printed on the paper form.

```
CREATE TABLE Timecards
(user_id CHAR(8) NOT NULL,
 punch_time TIMESTAMP DEFAULT CURRENT_TIMESTAMP NOT NULL,
 event_flag CHAR(3) DEFAULT 'IN ' NOT NULL
     CHECK(flag IN ('IN ', 'OUT')),
 PRIMARY KEY (user_id, punch_time));
```

But to answer even basic questions, you have to match up in and out times. Dr. Codd (1979) described a row in an RDBMS as containing a fact, but more than that, it should contain a whole fact and not half of it. The "half-fact" that John showed up at the job at 09:00 Hrs has nothing to do with paying him. I need to know that John was on the job from 09:00 to 17:00 Hrs. The correct design holds a whole in each row, thus:

```
CREATE TABLE Timecards
(user_id CHAR(8) NOT NULL,
 in_time TIMESTAMP DEFAULT CURRENT_TIMESTAMP NOT NULL,
 out_time TIMESTAMP,—null means current
 CHECK(in_time < out_time),
 PRIMARY KEY (user_id, in_time));
```

Many new SQL programmers are scared of NULLs, but this is a good use of them. We do not know the future, so we cannot assign a value to the out_time until we have that information.

Another common example is a simple order form that is copied directly into DDL. In skeleton form, the usual layout is something like this:

```
CREATE TABLE Orders
(order_nbr INTEGER NOT NULL PRIMARY KEY,
 ..
 order_total DECIMAL(12,2) NOT NULL,
 ..);

CREATE TABLE OrdersDetails
```

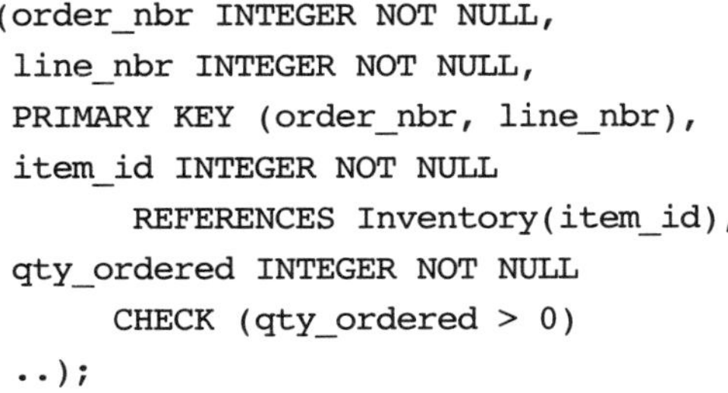

```
(order_nbr INTEGER NOT NULL,
 line_nbr INTEGER NOT NULL,
 PRIMARY KEY (order_nbr, line_nbr),
 item_id INTEGER NOT NULL
       REFERENCES Inventory(item_id),
 qty_ordered INTEGER NOT NULL
      CHECK (qty_ordered > 0)
 ..);
```

The order total can be computed from the order details, so it is redundant in the Orders table; but the total was a box on the paper form, so the newbie put it in the table.

Nobody is actually buying or shipping a line number. Customers are ordering items, but the lines on the paper form are numbered, so the line numbers are in the OrderDetails table. This is dangerous, because if I repeat the same item on another line, I have to consolidate them in the database. Otherwise, quantity discounts will be missed, and I am wasting storage with redundant data.

For example, each of the rows shows a "half-fact" in each row. One says that I ordered two pairs of lime green pants and the other says that I ordered three pairs of lime green pants on my order #123. The whole fact is that I ordered five pairs of lime green pants on my order #123.

In 2004, I pointed this out to a programmer who had such a schema. She insisted that they needed the line numbers to be able to reproduce the original order exactly as it was keyed in, but then in a following posting in the same thread, she complained that her people were spending hours every day verifying the quantity of items in orders they received, because their suppliers did not use the proper model to present a consolidated, sorted display of the data.

Resources

Military Standards

DoD 8320.1-M-1, Data Element Standardization Procedures.
DoD Directive 8320.1, "DoD Data Administration"

http://www.dtic.mil/whs/directives/corres/html/83201.htm
http://www.abelia.com/498pdf/498ARAPX.PDF

Metadata Standards

Here is a short summary of the NCITS L8 Metadata Standards Committee rules for data elements:

http://pueblo.lbl.gov/~olken/X3L8/drafts/draft.docs.html
http://lists.oasis-open.org/archives/ubl-ndrsc/200111/msg00005.html

Also the pdf file:
http://www.oasis-open.org/committees/download.php/6233/c002349_ISO_IEC_11179

The draft:
http://www.iso.org/iso/en/ittf/PubliclyAvailableStandards/c002349_ISO_IEC_11179-1_1999(E).zip

ANSI and ISO Standards

The SI Basics ("Metric System")

ISO 31 "Quantities and Units (14 parts)"

ISO 1000 "SI Units and Recommendations for the Use of Their Multiple and of Certain Other Units for the Application of the SI"

ISO 2955 "Information Processing—Representation of SI and Other Units for Use in Systems with Limited Character Sets"

A guide to both ISO 31 and ISO 1000 can be purchased at:

http://www.iso.org/iso/en/prods-services/prods-services/otherpubs/Quality.PublicationList?CLASSIFICATION=HANDBOOKS#090201

ISO 639-1:2002 "Codes for the Representation of Names of Languages—Part 1: Alpha-2 Code"

ISO 639-2:1998 "Codes for the Representation of Names of Languages—Part 2: Alpha-3 Code"

The language codes are available online:

http://www.loc.gov/standards/iso639-2/iso639jac.html

ISO 3166 "Codes for the Representation of Names of Countries"

This standard provides a unique two-letter code for each country and a three-letter code for special uses. A three-digit numeric code is given and intended as an alternative for all applications that need to be independent of the alphabet or to save bits in computer storage.

http://www.iso.org/iso/en/prods-services/popstds/countrynamecodes.html

ISO 4217:2001 "Codes for the Representation of Currencies and Funds"
http://www.iso.org/iso/en/prods-services/popstds/currencycodeslist.html

IBAN: International Standard Bank Number

http://www.ecbs.org/iban/iban.htm and the European Committee for Banking Standards Web site for publications

ISO 8601 "Data Elements and Interchange Formats—Information Interchange—Representation of Dates And Times."

http://www.iso.org/iso/en/prods-services/popstds/datesandtime.html

U.S. Government Codes

NAICS: North American Industry Classification System. This system replaced the old Standard Industrial Classification (SIC) system.

http://www.census.gov/epcd/www/naics.html

NAPCS: North American Product Classification System
http://www.census.gov/eos/www/napcs/napcs.htm

TIGER: Topologically Integrated Geographic Encoding and Referencing system. This is how the census views geography and reports data. It is available in electronic formats.

DOT: Dictionary of Occupational Titles. This is the U.S. Department of Labor encoding system. You can see some of the codes at this URL:

http://www.wave.net/upg/immigration/dot_index.html

Retail Industry

EAN: European Article Number, now combined with the UPC codes
ISO/IEC 15418:1999 "EAN/UCC Application Identifiers and Fact Data Identifiers and Maintenance"

ISO/IEC 15420:2000 "Automatic Identification and Data Capture Techniques—Bar Code Symbology Specification—EAN/UPC"

Bar Code Détente: U.S. Finally Adds One More Digit

2004 July 12, the *New York Times*, by Steve Lohr; http://www.nytimes.com/2004/07/12/business/12barcode.html?ex=1090648405&ei=1&en=202cb9baba72e846

VIN: Vehicle Identification Number
ISO 3779:1983 Vehicle Identification Number (VIN)

ISO 4030:1983 Vehicle Identification Number (VIN)—Location and Attachment

ISO/TR 8357:1996 Instructions for the implementation of the assignment of world manufacturer identifier (WMI) codes for vehicle identification number (VIN) systems and for world parts manufacturer identifier (WPMI) codes (available in English only)

A good news article on the changes that are coming to the VIN:

http://www.cars.com/news/stories/070104_storya_dn.jhtml?page=newsstory&aff=national

ISO tire sizes explained:

http://www.hostelshoppe.com/tech_tires.php

ISBN: International Standard Book Number
http://www.isbn.org/standards/home/index.asp

This site provides a converter for the new 13-digit ISBN that is based on the change from 10-digit UPC codes to 13-digit EAN codes in the retail industry on January 1, 2005.

Code Formatting and Naming Conventions

You can find other opinions at:

http://www.sqlservercentral.com/columnists/sjones/codingstandardspart2formatting.asp

http://www.sqlservercentral.com/columnists/sjones/codingstandardspart1formatting.asp.

Gulutzan, P. "SQL Naming Conventions," http://dbazine.com/gulutzan5.shtml

Bryzek, M. "Constraint Naming Standards," http://ccm.redhat.com/doc/core-platform/5.0/engineering-standards/eng-standards-constraint-naming-sect-1.html

Celko, J. "Ten Things I Hate about You," http://www.intelligententerprise.com/001205/celko1_1.jhtml?_requestid=304726

ISO/IEC. IS 11179-5 Information Technology Specification and Standardization of Data Elements: PART 5, Naming and Identification Principles for Data Elements.

http://metadata-standards.org/Document-library/Draft-standards/11179-Part5-Naming&Identification/

Jones, S. "Standards Part 1—Abbreviated Programming," http://www.databasejournal.com/features/mssql/article.php/1471461

Karbowski, J. J. "Naming Standards beyond Programming," http://www.devx.com/tips/Tip/12710

Koch, G., and K. Loney. *Oracle8i: The Complete Reference* (3rd ed.). Emeryville, CA: Osborne McGraw Hill, 2000.

Kondreddi, N., Vyas. "Database Object Naming Conventions," http://vyaskn.tripod.com/object_naming.htm

Mullins, C. "What's in a Name?" http://www.tdan.com/i004fe02.htm
Mullins, C. http://www.craigsmullins.com/dbt_0999.htm

Sheppard, S. "Oracle Naming Conventions," http://www.ss64.com/orasyntax/naming.html

Bibliography

Reading Psychology

Fisher, D. "Reading and Visual Search," *Memory and Cognition*, 3, 188-196, 1975.

Mason, M. "From Print to Sound in Mature Readers as a Function of Reader Ability and Two Forms of Orthographic Regularity," *Memory and Cognition*, 6, 568–581, 1978.

Meyer, D. E., and K. D. Gutschera. "Orthographic versus Phonemic Processing of Printed Words," Psychonomic Society Presentation, 1975.

Pollatsek, A., A. D. Well, and R. M. Schindler."Effects of Segmentation and Expectancy on Matching Time for Words and Nonwords," *Journal of Experimental Psychology: Human Perception and Performance*, 1, 328–338, 1975.

Saenger, P. *Space Between Words: The Origins of Silent Reading*. Palo Alto, CA: Stanford University Press, 1975.

Programming Considerations

Arthur, J. *Measuring Programmer Productivity and Software Quality*. New York: John Wiley & Sons, 1985.

Baecker, R. "Enhancing Program Readability and Comprehensibility with Tools for Program Visualization," *Proceedings of the 10th International Conference on Software Engineering*, 356-366, April 11-15, 1988, Singapore.

Berry, R. E., and A. E. Meekings. "A Style Analysis of C Programs," *Communications of the ACM*, 281, 80–88, January 1985.

Brooks, R. "Studying Programmer Behavior Experimentally: The Problems of Proper Methodology," *Communications of the ACM*, 234, 207–213, April 1980.

Celko, J. "Observations about Student Programming Practices," *Structured Programming*, Fall 1989, p. 215.

Celko, J. *SQL for Smarties* (3rd ed.). San Francisco: Morgan-Kaufmann, 2005.

Celko, J. *SQL Puzzles & Answers*. San Francisco: Morgan-Kaufmann, 1997.

Celko, J. *Data & Databases*. San Francisco: Morgan-Kaufmann, 1999.

Celko, J. *Trees & Hierarchies in SQL*. San Francisco: Morgan-Kaufmann, 2004.

Codd, E. F. "Extending the Database Relational Model to Capture More Meaning," *ACM Transactions on Database Systems*, 44, 397–434, December 1979.

Cooper, D., and M. J. Clancy. *Oh! Pascal*! New York: W. W. Norton, 1985.

Fairley, R. *Software Engineering Concepts*. Boston: McGraw-Hill, 1985.

Gilmore, D. J., and R. G. Green. "Comprehension and Recall of Miniature Programs," *International Journal of Man-Machine Studies*, 211, 31–48, July 1984.

Grogono, P. "On Layout, Identifiers and Semicolons in Pascal Programs," *ACM SIGPLAN Notices*, 14(4), 35-40, April 1979.

Kernighan, B., and P. J. Plauger. *The Elements of Programming Style*. Boston: McGraw-Hill, 1982.

Ledgard, H. *Programming Proverbs*. Rochelle Park, NJ, Hayden Books, 1975.

Ledgard, H., and L. J. Chmura. *Fortran with Style: Programming Proverbs*. Indianapolis, IN, Sams, 1978.

Ledgard, H., and J. Tauer. *Professional Software. Volume 2: Programming Practice*. Boston: Addison-Wesley Longman, 1987.

McCabe, Tom. "A Complexity Measure," *IEEE Transactions on Software*, 1976.

McKeithen, K., Reitman J., Rueter H., and Hirtle S. "Knowledge Organization and Skill Differences in Computer Programmers," *Cognitive Psychology*, 13, 307–325, 1981.

Meekings, B. "Style Analysis of Pascal Programs," *ACM SIGPLAN Notices*, 18(9), 45-54, September 1983.

Miller, G., A. "The Magical Number Seven Plus or Minus Two: Some Limits on Our Capacity for Processing Information," *The Psycological Review*, 1956.

Oman P., and Cook C. "A Taxonomy for Programming Style," *Proceedings of the 1990 ACM Annual Conference on Cooperation,* February 20–22, 1990, Washington, DC.

Oman P., and Cook C. "A Paradigm for Programming Style Research," *ACM SIGPLAN Notices*, 23(12), 69-78, December 1988.

Oman P., and Cook C. "Programming Style Authorship Analysis," *Proceedings of the 17th Annual ACM Conference on Computer Science:*

Computing Trends in the 1990s, Louisville, Kentucky, 320-326, February 1989

Oman P., and Cook C. "Typographic Style Is More Than Cosmetic," *Communications of the ACM*, 335, 506–520, May 1990.

Pascal, F. "SQL Redundancy and DBMS Performance," *Database Programming & Design,* 112, 22–28, December 1988.

Pressman, R. S. *Software Engineering: A Practitioner's Approach* (2nd ed.). Boston: McGraw-Hill, 1986.

Redish K., and Smyth W. "Program Style Analysis: A Natural By-Product of Program Compilation," *Communications of the ACM*, 29(2), 126-133, February 1986.

Rees, M. J. "Automatic Assessment Aids for Pascal Programs," *ACM SIGPLAN Notices*, 1710, 33–42, October 1982.

Sheil, B. A. "The Psychological Study of Programming," *ACM Computing Surveys* (CSUR), 131, 101–120, March 1981.

Weinberg, G. *The Psychology of Computer Programming: Silver Anniversary Edition*. New York: Dorset House, 1998.

Weissman, L. "Psychological Complexity of Computer Programs: An Experimental Methodology," *ACM SIGPLAN Notices*, 96, 25–36, June 1974.

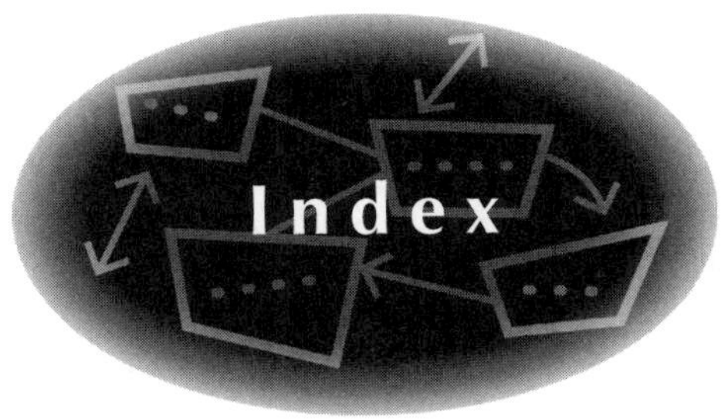

Index

ABOUT THE AUTHOR

Joe Celko is a noted consultant and lecturer, and one of the most-read SQL authors in the world. He is well known for his 10 years of service on the ANSI SQL standards committee, his column in *Intelligent Enterprise* magazine (which won several Reader's Choice Awards), and the war stories he tells to provide real-world insights into SQL programming. His best-selling books include *Joe Celko's SQL for Smarties: Advanced SQL Programming, second edition; Joe Celko's SQL Puzzles and Answers;* and *Joe Celko's Trees and Hierarchies in SQL for Smarties.*